CHASING COVERED BRIDGES

CHASING COVERED BRIDGES

AND
How to Find Them

By Paul Parrott

Publishing Company
Nashville, Tennessee

www.turnerpublishing.com

Copyright © 2005 Turner Publishing Company

No part of this book may be reproduced or transmitted in
any form or by any means, electronic or mechanical,
including photocopying, recording, or by any information
storage and retrieval system, without permission in
writing from the publisher.

Turner Publishing Company Staff:
Keith Steele: Publishing Consultant
Charlotte Harris: Project Coordinator

Library of Congress Control No.
2005927922

ISBN: 978-1-68162-545-4

0 9 8 7 6 5 4 3 2 1

Acknowledgments

My wife, Dee, without whose love and help I could not have hunted and found these hundreds of bridges. My entire family and so many friends who finally convinced me that somehow I could plan and write this book. My deceased friend, Jimmy Shepherd, whose interest in the Kentucky covered bridges helped to get me started on this wonderful journey. To God Almighty who provided me with health, finances, and so graciously provided us with safe passage throughout thousands of miles of travel. And to the National Society for Preservation of Covered Bridges for so graciously allowing me to use their *World Guide to Covered Bridges* in preparing the how to find section of this book.

Table of Contents

Acknowledgments v
Introduction ix
Words and Abbrevations xi
Truss Types xi
The Hunt 3
Bridges
    Alabama 14
    California 16
    Connecticut 18
    Delaware 19
    Georgia 20
    Illinois 22
    Indiana 25
    Iowa 46
    Kentucky 49
    Maine 52
    Maryland 54
    Massachusetts 56
    Michigan 57
    Minnesota 58
    Missouri 59
    New Hampshire 61
    New Jersey 66
    New York 67
    North Carolina 71
    Ohio 72
    Oregon 89
    Pennsylvania 98
    South Carolina 130
    Tennessee 131
    Vermont 132
    Virginia 149
    Washington 151
    West Virginia 152
    Wisconsin 155
Guides & Maps 158
Covered Bridges of the United States 159
Index 228

Introduction

As I view these proud old structures, I can almost feel that I am reliving a lot of the past history of our great country. They represent a very important time in the growth and development of the America we love, enjoy and often just seem to take for granted. It is my sincere hope that I can somehow help all who read this, and those who as a result of the reading take more time to really see and appreciate not just the covered bridges of which I write, but also the greatness of our entire country. No source of information on the bridges is rarely entirely completely correct, but so nearly so as to enable me to find over eight hundred.

Words and Abbrevations

OPEN - in use for vehicular traffic

CLOSED - closed to all but foot traffic

BUILT - where records of dates of completion are known

Truss Types

K.P. - king post

MKP - multiple king post

BURR or ARCH - trusses with supporting arches

QP - queen post

SMITH - name of truss designer

LONG - name of truss designer

HOWE - name of truss designer

PADDLEFORD - name of truss designer

WARREN - name of truss designer

PDLFD - paddleford

The Hunt

In 1991, I photographed my first covered bridge by chance while traveling inland from the Oregon coast to Crater Lake National Park. This was of little interest to me at the time. Sometime later a friend who was interested in covered bridges, especially in Kentucky, got me slightly interested in the structures, and I joined the now defunct **Kentucky Covered Bridges Association**. In 1994 while searching the *Rand McNally Atlas* for points of interest to see on one of our many trips west, I noticed a red dot and the words covered bridges on the Madison County section of the Iowa map. We detoured to the Winterset area and they were celebrating the filming of the movie, **The Bridges of Madison County**. I took photos of five, but somehow missed the Roseman covered bridge which was the prime source of the story. Quite frankly I was just as interested in John Wayne's boyhood home in Winterset as I was in the covered bridges at that time, but the seed of interest had been planted. In 1996 I had a severe bout with depression and anxiety and during the recovery period I started phoning various state tourism bureaus and from or through them gained a fair amount of information from those that had covered bridges and their locations and started planning trips. Starting in February 1997 starting in Kentucky, Indiana, Alabama, Georgia, North Carolina, South Carolina, Tennessee, Ohio, New York, Connecticut, Vermont, New Hampshire, Massachusetts, and Maine ending in Pennsylvania in early October with a total of approximately 210 covered bridges seen and photographed, several

Brookwood C.B. near Arcata County, CA Humboldt, County, CA, open Howe built 1969.

The Hunt

instances of interest occurred. During these trips, once in Indiana, we arrived at a very nice bridge during early morning fog. While waiting for the fog to clear enough to get a photo, a situation with all the appearance of a drug deal developed, but no one seemed concerned by or with us. While searching for another Indiana bridge, the road signs were just steel posts with numbers, which were often bent and twisted, so it was not easy to decide which gravel road to take causing us to get quite lost with no one in sight to ask directions. After passing the same little burg three times, Dee (my wife) said "Paul if we go through here one more time they will require us to take up residence." We did, however, find someone who could direct us. When we found it I said "Aha! There you are," and told Dee it seemed to say "Where have you been? I've been waiting for you." Something I would repeat many times the next few years. Once in Vermont, we were lost while looking for a certain bridge. We stopped at a quick stop station. I asked the attendant if he knew where this bridge was by name. His answer was "yes" he knew there was one close by but up here they are kind of like ladies of the night and we don't pay a lot of attention to them. We arrived in Maine on the last weekend of September when the leaves were just getting in full color. We

Red C.B. Princeton, IL Bureau County, IL Howe built 1863.

Spencerville C.B. DeKalb County, IN open Howe built 1873.

had planned to stay a day or two at Bar Harbor, but everywhere we called they were full up. We stayed at a little motel up in the hills and started back toward New York the next morning looking for a place to stay. Finally at St. Albans, Vermont the Cadillac Motel attendant said all she had left was the bridal suite with red décor and lots of mirrors. We decided this was not for a couple like us in our seventies. So she said well we could have her quarters but would have to be in before 11 p.m. and could not leave before 7 a.m., as the lobby would be locked. This was fine with us. The leaves are really beautiful in New England in the fall but it is best to have advance accommodations reserved. During 1998 and 1999 we made many trips to Indiana, Ohio, Maryland, Virginia, West Virginia, Pennsylvania, Delaware, Illinois, Iowa, Wisconsin, Minnesota, Michigan, Washington, Oregon, California. Another trip to New York, Vermont, New Hampshire and a short trip into Quebec, Canada. We arrived at the border before 8:00 a.m. I am a early riser. Signs at the Canadian Station stated we could check in at either one of two towns. When the border station was not manned, we found one of them and was told we would need to go to the other. So I told Dee we would just go back to the USA and come back after 8:00 a.m, which we did. After talking to a very friendly guard at the Canadian station. I told him what we had done and he said uh oh, they will be looking for you. We had been caught on camera going both ways. He advised us to also go back and get cleared at the U.S. station. A very amused attendant was expecting us and cleared us as did the Canadian station. We returned into Quebec and found the five covered bridges we were looking for and had an uneventful trip. Later on this trip in New Hampshire we went to a golf course in Keene, New Hampshire which has seven stringer type covered bridges. They let me use a golf cart to see and photo some of them. Sprinklers were going full force and needless to say I got pretty well drenched. Later that same day, kind of lost again, we stopped at a roadside business of some kind for directions. A very shaggy and very old looking dog was just lying there until I got out of the car. Then he acted really vicious. As I slowly backed into my car, a man nearby said he was just there to fix something and had no knowledge of the dog or the covered bridge I was seeking but it might be just ahead. It was, and a fairly new one. I almost forgot, back in Ohio a very nice pretty little red and black snake wanted to share a bridge with me. Harmless I am sure, only to me there is no such thing as a harmless snake. In 2001 we took another trip into Pennsylvania. Photographed 93 covered bridges for a total of 219 in Pennsylvania. It was early May and all very green and in bloom. A man in Jefferson County has a small covered bridge on his property built to specifications. Very nice and a friendly fellow. Would have talked all day I believe. Our latest trip was back to Washington, Oregon, and California for 35 covered bridges and one each in Missouri and Illinois for the grand total of 802. I have hopes for another trip to

Hogback C.B. Madison County, IA closed Town, built 1884.

Pennsylvania, New York, Connecticut, Massachusetts, New Hampshire, Vermont, Maine, for the ones missed on earlier trips and perhaps a short trip to New Brunswick, Canada to get the Hartland covered bridge, which is the world's longest at 1282 feet.

In Chester County, Pennsylvania there are two covered bridges in the Laurel Preserve of the Brandywine Conservancy. You need permission and an escort to photo them. Through many phone calls I finally located a fellow who would meet me there. Never could reach him by phone but after arriving in Pennsylvania, left a message on his answering machine as to the day, hour and spot I would meet him and almost to the minute he was there and I got to photo both bridges.

Throughout all these trips we met a lot of friendly helpful

people. In Vermont a man and his son were doing lawn work. He said he would let his son take his car and take me to the bridge I was seeking. His directions seemed so good that I declined and we found it okay. It was our 600th covered bridge. Again in Indiana I was asking directions at a quick stop. A man standing near by heard and said just follow him when he left and he would take me directly to it. Which he did. If you start seriously chasing covered bridges you should be prepared to be lost pretty often. Roads that used to have a number now have a name or vice versa. Or simply no sign at all. Or the road is sometimes named the same as the bridge or the same name as the stream it spans or just covered bridge road. You may also see signs stating load limit three tons or on occasion higher limits or clearance overhead of 8 - 10 feet or slightly higher. Almost all bridges have names but not all have the name on the portal. Hunting covered bridges is by no means an exact science so to speak. Persistence and determination is a valuable asset. I have driven up to 30 - 40 extra miles to find a bridge and it was always a thrill when I located it. Each one to me has its own personality and attraction. Some so proud and stately and others downtrodden and abused with neglect, deterioration and graffiti. Many are in use every day. Others are in parks or simply bypassed and standing in various stages of repair close to a concrete or steel bridge. All that are recognized by the **National Society for the Preservation of Covered Bridges** are supported by various types and combinations of tension and compression trusses of wood and steel or just wood with supporting upper and lower chords. The roofs have their own supporting systems and along with the siding planks to protect the supporting trusses and flooring from the elements. Not being an engineer, I will go no further into the construction technology except to say that replacing the roof and sides is far more economical than replacing the trusses, chords and flooring.

Colville C.B. Bourbon County, KY open MKP, (rebuilt and opened 2001).

Many theories have been proposed as to why the bridges are covered. Some say it was so lovers could have privacy. Others say it was easier to keep horses and mules from being frightened and perhaps hurting themselves or their passengers. As I more or less stated earlier, it was simply a matter of economics and protection of supporting timber from the elements. This is not to say that courting and spooning did not occur. Several were either actually named or called kissing bridges (on more than one occasion Dee and I stole a quick kiss while passing through). They also served as community bulletin boards, places for family picnics, political rallies, weddings, church services, hiding places for robbers and it has been said that persons desiring a little "bootleg" moonshine would place his money in a designated slot and return later to find a bottle in its place. Oh yes, on one occasion here in Kentucky when the Colville covered bridge had been repaired and reopened to traffic I took my wife Dee and two other ladies to see it and casually mentioned that some are known as kissing bridges and all three got out and walked through. Can't imagine why!! These grand old structures also served during the Civil War. Also many were lost during that period. Over the years arson and floods have destroyed hundreds. In Ohio which once had well over 3000, the flood of 1913 resulted in millions of dollars lost in bridges. Many of which were covered bridges. Today Ohio has about 140, several which have been built in the 1990s. Pennsylvania once had well over 1000. Today about 220 remain. From day to day it is difficult to state an exact number of those left in the U.S. due to losses from arson and floods. But the number is about 880. I would like to see the 80 more or less that I have not seen. But my age, 78, and miles of travel

Hancock Greenfield C.B. Hillsborough County, NH open Pratt built unknown.

The Hunt

Eaglesville C.B. Washington County, NY open Town built 1858.

involved make it doubtful that I will succeed. The latest list published by the NSPCB lists two new ones in New York, one in Connecticut and one in Massachusetts. But I digress. The earliest bridges were logs or tree felled across a stream. Then two logs with planks as a floor. Those did not support a lot of weight nor did they last long, hence the development of the truss and chord system and protective covering. Sometimes they were toll bridges. Also many were railroad bridges. Two of these still exist in Vermont and possibly one in Oregon and one in New Hampshire. There could be others of which I am not aware. Sometimes when traveling circuses wanted to pass through covered bridges they were turned away because they did not have sufficient knowledge of an elephants weight or the weight the bridge could support. Horses were forbidden to run across these bridges as it was believed the vibration could cause the bridge to collapse. Some still bear this sign - *Cross this bridge at a walk or pay $? fine* (some say $1 others $5). The longest ever built in the U.S. was 5690 feet long across the Susquehanna River at Columbia, Pennsylvania, supported by 28 stone piers. I have no knowledge of when or how it was lost. Currently the longest in the U.S. is the Cornish/Windsor covered bridge over the Connecticut River connecting New Hampshire and Vermont, 460 feet long and open to traffic, a true

The Hunt

work of art to me. Kentucky presently has 13 truss covered bridges and at least four stringer or otherwise known as a labor of love of which there are many. A lot of which are shown in the Reiman Publications "Life in the Slow Lane" published a few years past. As we have traveled to 31 states that have these treasures of the past, we have seen so much of the back country. Beautiful hills, mountains, plains and streams far removed from the hustle and bustle of the cities and towns. Peaceful and quiet. So much so in fact that sometimes there is quite a drive without stores or gas stations so be sure to avail yourself of all rest stops when you come upon one. Sometimes you see very few people for long periods of time, but invariably they are friendly and helpful. Be sure to have water and snacks with you as restaurants are not plentiful and plan ahead for a place to stay each night. And keep an eye on your fuel gauge. Also, I always have a written map of all roads involved each day so Dee can keep me on track. Even so sometimes when kind of lost, we disagree on which road is right. But it is all fun and we get there. You can too if you avail yourself of all the information I will provide later in this book. Nationwide there has been a welcome trend of repair and restoration of these structures that played such a vital role in the development of our country. I really believe that increased interest by people like you and I has been and will continue to be instrumental in this trend continuing and perhaps gaining momentum in the future.

Doyle Road C.B. Ashtabula County, OH Town & Arch built 1876.

Before you start any tour, search your maps and all other resources for other points of interest on or close to your route. In another section, I will endeavor to provide all the available information I have that I believe will be helpful to you. I have not written anything of my prior life. If you will bear with me a moment I will say I grew up on a farm (no covered bridge) in west central Kentucky, went in the Navy in 1943, retired from the same in 1966. I then worked for close to twenty years for the U.S. Postal Service, retired from that in 1986. Dee kind of urged me to take a third career, but I declined and we just traveled a lot. She and I married in 1964, me almost 40 and she 35, had two children and have four grandchildren. Our son is also career Navy, our daughter a stay at home mom. Since I have not attempted to write this in a well organized format, I would like to say yes I hope for some financial gain. I also have a strong hope that I may help increase personal, state, and national interest in the preservation of and the pleasure of seeing this wonderful part of our history. As I walk or slowly drive through them or stand on the banks, I can almost hear the sounds of children playing and the sounds of horse drawn vehicles passing through. Baptisms were another event that often took place near by. On our last trip to Pennsylvania, we witnessed such an event taking place in the stream near a covered bridge. This is one more thing that is long past history and it brought back the memory of my own baptism in the old swimming hole. As you travel you will encounter many relics from the past. Take your time and enjoy our great country. Almost forgot - as we were photographing a covered bridge in New Hampshire a couple was taking pictures. Thinking they shared our interest, I approached them and it turned out they were from Washington and were married on that bridge a couple of years earlier. Quite a few apparently still serve this purpose. Met a fellow in Vermont one day touring part of the state on a bicycle. For the next few hours it was nip and tuck as to which of us got to the next bridge. He volunteered to take my photo with my camera. Just another of the things that add to the adventure of covered bridging. I should add that I am not a purist. I have photographed several that are not of historical value and are not constructed as a truss bridge but

Office C.B. Lane County, OR open Howe built 1944 (perhaps the tallest in the U.S.).

they serve peoples needs and are covered so I simply could not pass them up and not include them. Another item of interest to me and Dee was when we did visit the Roseman covered bridge in Madison County, Iowa they had a book for sale at the gift shop near by titled **"Covered Bridge Ghost Stories."** I did not purchase it. Went on to California, Oregon, and Washington. Kept thinking about it. Returning home on I-80, I kept trying to decide if I would return to Madison County, Iowa and buy it. About 15 miles before reaching the exit to Winterset, our right front tire blew out. Put on the spare tire, went on to Winterset where I could get a new tire. Next morning, went back to the gift shop and got the book. It is very good and I recommend it. Author Karen Zweifel ISBN 1-88154-23-6. Are covered bridges really haunted? Who can say? If these ghost

The Hunt

stories are hard to prove they are equally hard to disprove. Personally, I just let my imagination take over as I drive or walk through or around them. I can conjure up all sorts of scenarios. On another occasion in New York, when we arrived at the bridge we were seeking, a group of what appeared to be teenagers were partying in it. They were not inclined to leave but stood lined up along one side and except for some mild hand slapping on the car we slowly passed through, then stopped and took a photo with some of them getting in the picture. If you enjoy waterfalls as we do, there are lots of them out there and a little research can add a lot of pleasure to your journey. You may ask has my wife, Dee, shared my enthusiasm in all this chasing covered bridges. In the beginning for her it was mostly the joy of traveling and sight seeing. But gradually she started to also enjoy the hunt. Enough so that if a bridge was so difficult to find that I was about ready to give up she urged me on. When you undertake a journey such as we did, it truly takes mutual support and sharing of the joys and disappointments (and yes there were some let downs). We both feel very blessed that we have been spiritually, financially, and physically able to travel and see all that we have with no accidents or mishaps greater than two flat tires. The National Society for the Preservation of Covered Bridges (NSPCB) publishes a quarterly bulletin and newsletter that I find very valuable and interesting. Cost is included in membership fees. Back copies are available for a very reasonable fee. If you have an interest in what is happening in all or various states I highly recommend joining this organization. Also several states have covered bridge societies or associations. Ohio has a historical bridge association that includes

New Baltimore C.B. Somerset County, PA open MKP built 1879 and rebuilt 1990s.

The Hunt

Creamery C.B. Windham County, VT open Town built 1879.

covered bridges. Several have annual festivals. I will share some of this information that I have later in the how to find section of this book. I sincerely hope many who read this will find pleasure and fun as we have done. I have been asked why most of my photos are either directly facing the portals or a portal and a side view. In part it was a matter of the terrain or having to get in or almost in the stream. But primarily I just do not prefer side views, it's kind of like taking a side view of a friend. We just returned from a southern tour where we viewed a few good waterfalls, visited our son and his family for a great week. Also photographed two covered bridges previously missed, the old Union/Talahatchee in Dekalb County, Alabama. A very nice bridge and open for traffic. The Lula/Blind in Banks County, Georgia is a pitiful sight of neglect, but still standing defiant and proud. We also found out that the Nector covered bridge in Blount County, Alabama was burned several years past by vandals who apparently had been arrested for drug use in or about the bridge. Also the one I had thought still remained in Mississippi has either been destroyed or moved to private property. No one seemed sure which. Also the Wehadkee covered bridge in the Calloway Gardens Harris County, Georgia remains banned for public view. An employee did take a picture and sent me an 8x10 computer enhanced copy. All in all I have been reminded of so many cases of sad neglect and the need for public awareness of the historical value of these grand old structures, many of which still serve community needs on a daily basis. Several times in writing this narrative I have felt I had reached the closing point. Once again I feel that further writing would perhaps become just repetition, so I sincerely wish you safe trips and happy covered bridging.

                                                    Paul

Alabama

Al Horton C.B. Blount County, AL, open lattice Town built 1934.

Talahatchee/Old Union C.B. DeKalb County, AL, open MKP built-date unknown.

Al Swann C.B. Blount County, AL, Town lattice built 1933.

Alabama

Easter C.B. Blount County, AL open Town lattice built 1927.

Liddy Walker C.B. Cullman County, AL open Town built unknown.

Waldo/Riddle Mill C.B. Talladega County, AL closed Howe & QP built 1858.

Gilland C.B. Etowah County, AL closed Town built 1899.

Coldwater C.B. Calhoun County, AL open MKP built 1850.

Clarkson C.B. Cullman County, AL closed Town built 1904.

Salem Shotwell C.B. Lee County, AL closed Town built 1900.

California

Castleberry C.B. Cherokee, CA, Butte County, CA Warren built 1984.

Wanowa C.B. Mariposa County, CA, closed Warren built 1875 (being repaired) This was my 800th covered bridge.

Bridgeport C.B. near Nevada City, CA in Nevada County closed Howe & Arch built 1862. (side view) "Yankee Jim" reportedly was hung there and later found to be innocent.

California

Knights Ferry C.B. Staneslous County, CA, closed built 1864.

Freemans Crossing C.B. Yuba County, CA, open QP built 1862.

Honey Run C.B. Butte County, CA closed Pratt built 1896.   *Bertas Ranch C.B. Humboldt County, CA open QP built 1936.*

Connecticut

West Cornwall C.B. Litchfield County, CT open Burr built 1841.

Bulls Bridge C.B. Litchfield County, CT open QP & Town built 1842.

Delaware

Ashland C.B. New Castle County, DE open Town built 1870.

Woodale C.B. New Castle, County, DE open Town built 1870.

Georgia

Euharlee C.B. Bartow County, GA closed Town built 1890. #2

Stone Mountain C.B. DeKalb County, GA open Town built 1893.

Haralson C.B. Rockdale County, GA open Town steel & concrete deck, built 1990s.

Georgia

Coheelee C.B. Early County, GA closed QP built 1883.

Concord C.B. Cobb County, GA open QP built 1872 (on a very busy street in Symrna, GA).

Pools Mill C.B. Forsythe County, GA closed Town built 1906.

Watson Mill C.B. Madison/Oglethorpe Counties open Town lattice built 1885.

Big Red Oak C.B. Meriweather County, GA closed Town built 1840.

Elders Mill C.B. Oconee County, GA closed Town built 1897.

Illinois

Lake of the Woods C.B. Champaign County, IL open modern concrete & steel.

Greenup C.B. Cumberland County, IL, open Burr built 2000 (modified).

Centennial C.B. DuPage County, IL Long built 1981 (foot traffic only).

Illinois

Riverwalk Foot C.B. DuPage County, IL open Long built 1987.

Alaman or Eames C.B. Henderson County, IL closed Burr & Arch built 1865.

Illinois

Wolf C.B., Knox County, IL open Howe built 1874, destroyed & rebuilt in 1990s.

Little Mary's C. B. near Chester, IL, Randolph County, IL closed Burr built 1854.

Glenarm C.B. Sangamon County, IL closed MKP Arch built 1880.

Thompson Mill C.B. Shelby County, IL closed Howe built 1868.

Indiana

Ceylon C.B. Adams County, IN closed Howe built 1862.

Ramp Creek C.B. Brown County, IN open Burr built 1838, (two-lane).

Lancaster C.B. Carroll County, IN open Howe built 1872.

Indiana

Guilford C.B. Dearborn County, IN open Burr built 1879.

Westport C.B. Decatur County, IN closed Burr built 1880.

Longwood C.B. Fayette County, IN, closed MKP & arch built 1884.

Indiana

Aqueduct C.B. Franklin County, IN open Burr, open Burr built 1846 (to water traffic) (very rare type).

Cumberland C.B. Grant County, IN open Howe built 1877.

Cedar Chapel C.B. Hamilton County, IN, open Howe built 1884.

Indiana

Medora C.B. Jackson County, IN closed Burr built 1875. (Said to be longest in U.S.? Not so, it is second to the Cornish/Windsor, VT-NH).

James C.B. Jennings County, IN open Howe built 1887.

Sepio C.B. Jennings County, IN open Howe built 1886

Indiana

Fairgrounds C.B. Lake County, IN, open MKP & Arch built 1878. (Also known as Milroy/Crown Point).

Deersmill C.B. Montgomery County, IN closed Burr built 1878.

Cataract Falls C.B. Owen County, IN closed Smith built 1876.

Indiana

Beeson C.B. Parke County, IN open Burr built 1906.

Billie Creek C.B. Parke County, IN open Burr built 1895.

Bridgton C.B. Parke County, IN closed Burr built 1868.

Indiana

Catlin C.B. Parke County, IN closed Burr built 1907.

Cox Ford C.B. Parke County, IN open Burr built 1913.

Crooks Bridge C.B. Parke County, IN open Burr built 1895.

Indiana

Leatherwood C.B. Parke County, IN open Burr built 1899.

Mansfield C.B. Parke County, IN, open Burr built 1867.

Marshall C.B. Parke County, IN open Burr built 1917.

Indiana

Mecca C.B. Parke County, IN closed Burr built 1873 (later opened).

Melcher C.B. Parke County, IN open Burr built 1896.

Narrows Bridge Parke County, IN open Burr built 1882.

Indiana

Phillips C.B. Parke County, IN open MKP, built 1909.

Portland Mills C.B. Parke County, IN open Burr built 1887.

Rush Creek C.B. Parke County, IN open Burr built 1904.

Indiana

Sam Smith C.B. Parke County, IN open Burr built 1883.

Nevins C.B. Parke County, IN, open Burr built 1920.

Zacks Cox C.B. Parke County, IN, open Burr built 1908.

Indiana

Bakers Camp C.B. Putnam County, IN, open Burr built 1901.

Cornstalk C.B. Putnam County, IN, open Burr built 1917.

Dunbar C.B. Putnam County, IN open Burr built 1880.

Indiana

Hoeck C.B. Putnam County, IN open Howe built 1884.

Oakkalla C.B. Putnam County, IN open Burr built 1898.

Rolling Stone C.B. Putnam County, IN open Burr built 1915.

Indiana

Holton C.B. Ripley County, IN closed Howe built 1884.

Forsythe C.B. Rush County, IN open Burr built 1888.

Moscow C.B. Rush County, IN open Burr built 1886.

Indiana

Norris Ford C.B. Rush County, IN open Burr built 1916.

Smith C.B. Rush County, IN closed Burr built 1877.

Huffman Mill C.B. Spencer County, IN (Perry County), open Burr built 1864.

Indiana

Hillsdale C.B. Vermillion County, IN closed Burr built 1875 (in Ernie Pyle Rest Park).

Newport C.B. Vermillion County, IN open Burr built 1885.

North Manchester C.B. Wabash County, IN closed Smith built 1872.

Indiana

Roann C.B. Wabash County, IN open Howe built 1847.

New Brownsville C.B. Bartholemew County, IN Millrose Park, Columbus, IN open Long built 1840.

Bean Blosson C.B. Brown County, IN open Howe built 1880.

Cades Mill C.B. Fountain County, IN closed Howe built 1854.

Indiana

Rob Roy C.B. Fountain County, IN open Howe built 1860.

Snow Hill C.B. Franklin County, IN open Howe built 1894.

Old Red C.B. Gibson County, IN closed Smith built 1875.

Richland Creek C.B. Greene County, IN open Burr built 1883.

Potters C.B. Hamilton County, IN closed Howe built 1871.

Vermont C.B. Howard County, IN closed Smith built 1875.

Shieldstown C.B. Jackson County, IN closed Burr built 1876.

Williams C.B. Lawrence County, IN open Howe truss built 1884.

Indiana

Darlington C.B. Montgomery County, IN closed built 1868.

Sanatorium C.B. Parke County, IN open Burr built 1910, (Note: open for private use by santorium personnel only).

Neet C.B. Parke County, IN closed Burr built unknown.

Thorpe Ford C.B. Parke County, IN closed Burr built 1912.

Roseville C.B. Parke County, IN open Burr built 1910.

Big Rocky Fork C.B. Parke County, IN closed Burr built 1900.

Mill Creek C.B. Parke County, IN open Burr built 1907.

Wilkies Mill C.B. Parke County, IN open Burr built 1906.

Indiana

Jeffries Ford C.B. Parke County, IN open Burr built 1915 (burned April 3, 1915).

Conleys C.B. Parke County, IN open Burr built 1907.

Harry Evan C.B. Parke County, IN open Burr built 1908.

McAllisters Bridge C.B. Parke County, IN open Burr built 1914.

Bowsher C.B. Parke County, IN open Burr built 1915.

Jackson C.B. Parke County, IN open Burr built 1861.

Pine Bluff C.B. Putnam County, IN open Howe built unknown.

Indiana

Edna Collins C.B. Putnam County, IN open Burr built 1922.

Huffman C.B. Putnam County, IN open Howe built 1880.

Busching C.B. Ripley County, IN open Howe built 1885.

Offutt's C.B. Rush County, IN open Burr built 1884.

Leota C.B. Scott County, IN open concrete and steel modern type built 1990s.

Eugene C.B. Vermillion County C.B. closed Burr built 1885.

Irishman C.B. Vigo County, IN closed QP built 1847 (in Fowler Park).

West Union C.B. Parke County, IN closed Burr built 1876.

Iowa

Cedar C.B. Madison County, IA Town open built 1883. (burned 2003).

Cutler Donahoe C.B. Madison County, IA closed Burr built 1869.

Iowa

Holliwell C.B. Madison County, Winterset, IA closed Town & Arch built 1880.

Roseman C.B. Madison County, Winterset, IA, closed Town built 1883. (This is not the movie bridge).

Hammond C.B. Marion County, IA open Howe built 1883.

Iowa

Pioneer Park C.B. Cerro Gordo County, IA closed Town built 1969.

Delta C.B. Keokuk County, IA Burr closed built 1869.

Imes C.B. Madison County, IA closed Town built 1871.

Game Reserve C.B. Marion County, IA open Town built 1891.

Old Marysville C.B. Marion County, IA closed Town built 1891.

Owens C.B. Polk County, IA closed Howe built 1888.

Kentucky

Walcot/White C.B. Braken County, KY, closed MK & QP built 1880, (rebuilt 2001).

Goddard/White C.B. Fleming County, KY Town Lattice built date-unknown.

Kentucky

Switer C.B. Franklin County, KY closed Howe, built 1855, (completely rebuilt after 1997 flood).

Dover C.B. Mason County, KY QP built 1835.

Beech Fork/Mooresville C.B. Washington County, KY built 1865, closed.

Kentucky

Johnson Creek C.B. Robertson County, KY closed Howe built 1874.

Hillsboro C.B. Fleming County, KY closed MKP built 1867.

Oldtown C.B. Greenup County, KY closed MKP built 1870.

Ringos Mill C.B. Fleming County, KY MKP built 1867.

Bennetts Mill C.B. Greenup County, KY open Long built 1855.

Maine

#1 Bennett Bean C.B. Cumberland County, ME Paddleford built 1901.

Hemlock C.B. Cumberland County, ME open Paddleford built 1867.

Maine

Love Joy C.B. Cumberland County, ME Paddleford built 1867.

Sunday River C.B. Cumberland County, ME Paddleford built 1870.

Maryland

Jerico C.B. Baltimore/Hackford County, Kingsville, MD Burr built 1858.

Roddy Creek C.B. Frederick County, MD near Thurmond, MD open KP built 1850.

Utica C.B. Frederick County, MD near Thurmont, MD open MKP built 1850.

Maryland

Gilpins C.B. Cecil County, MD Burr closed built 1860.

Black Bridge C.B. Cecil County, MD Burr open built 1860, (near Appleton, MD Fox Catehor Farm).

Loys Station C.B. Frederick County, MD open MKP built 1880.

Massachusetts

Bissell C.B. Franklin County, MA closed Long built 1957.

Service C.B. Worcester County, MA Burr closed built.

Vermont C.B. Worcester County, MA closed Smith built 1870.

Michigan

Zehnder C.B. Saginaw County, MI Town open built 1980 (two-lane).

Ada C.B. Kent County, MI closed Howe built 1980.

Fallsburg C.B. Kent County, MI open Brown built 1871.

Whites C.B. Ionia County, MI open Brown built 1896.

Minnesota

Zumbroto C.B., Goodloe County, MN, Zumbroto, MN closed built 1869 (only covered bridge in Minnesota)

Missouri

Sandy Creek C.B. Jefferson County, MO near Hillsboro, MO Howe built 1886.

Union C.B. Monroe County, MO near Paris, MO closed Burr built 1871.

Langley C.B. St. Joseph County, MO open Howe built 1887.

Bollinger Mill C.B. Cape Girardeau County, MO closed Howe built 1868.

Locust Creek C.B. Linn County, MO closed Howe built 1868.

New Hampshire

Barlett C.B. Carroll County, NH closed Paddleford built 1870 (has shop in it).

Conway Saco River C.B. Carroll County NH open Burr built 1890.

Jackson Honeymoon C.B. Carroll County, NH open Burr built 1876.

New Hampshire

Conway Saco River C.B. closed Burr built 1870, (met a couple who got married here three years earlier).

Cresson/Sawyer C.B. Cheshire County, NH Town open built 1859.

Swanzey/Carleton C.B. Cheshire County, NH QP open built 1869.

New Hampshire

Thompson C.B. Cheshire County, NH Town open built 1832.

Upper Village C.B. Cheshire County, NH open lattice built 1864.

Stark/Stark C.B. Coos County, NH open Long & Arch built 1863.

New Hampshire

Bath/Bath C.B. Grafton County, NH. open Burr built unknown.

Swiftwater C.B. Grafton County, NH open Burr built 1849.

Cornish Windsor C.B. Sullivan, County, NH, (connects NH-VT), Windsor County, VT open lattice-type built 1866.

Cornish Windsor C.B. connects NH-VT Sullivan County, NH, Windsor County, VT built 1866.

New Hampshire

Drewsville C.B. Sullivan County, NH open Town built 1869.

McDermott C.B. Sullivan County, NH closed Town built 1869.

Haverhill C.B. Grafton County, NH open Town & Arch built 1827.

Albany/Albany C.B. Carroll County, NH open Paddleford built 1858.

Newport Corbin C.B. Sullivan County, NH open Town built 1835.

New Jersey

Green Sergeants C. B./Hunterdon C.B. QP open built 1866, (only one in state).

New York

Fitches C.B. Delaware County, NY Town open built 1870.

Salisbury Ctr. C.B. Herkimer County, NY open KP & Arch built 1875 (teenagers were partying).

Buskirks C.B. Rensselaer/Washington Counties, NY open Howe built 1880.

New York

Blenheim C.B. Schoharie County, NY closed Smith built 1855 (rare two-lane).

Beaverkill/Conklin C.B. Sullivan County, NY Town open built 1865.

Chestnut Creek C.B. Sullivan County, NY Town open built unknown (two-lane).

New York

Vantran/Livingston C.B. Sullivan County, NY Town open built 1860.

Newfield C.B. Tompkins County, NY open Town built 1853.

Rexleigh C.B. Washington County, NY open Howe built 1874.

New York

Hamden C.B. Delaware County, NY open Long built 1859.

Downsville C.B. Delaware County, NY open Long & QP built 1854.

Americana Village C.B. Madison County, NY closed Warren private built 1968.

Allegany Park C.B. Stringer County, NY foot traffic only steel reinforced built c1990s.

Grants Mill C.B. Ulster County, NY closed Town built 1902.

Shushan C.B. Washington County, NY closed Town built 1858 (used as museum and library).

North Carolina

Pisgah C.B. Randolph County, NC (Stringer) closed built 1910.

Ohio

Netcher C.B. Ashtabula County, OH open Haupt built 1999.

Blackwood C.B. Athens County OH open MKP built 1881.

New Hope C.B. Brown County, OH closed Howe Arch built 1878.

Ohio

Mantinsville C.B. Clinton County, OH open MKP built 1871.

Helmick C.B. Coshocton County, OH open MKP built 1863.

Hizey C.B. Fairfield County, OH open MKP & Arch built 1891.(on private drive).

Ohio

Rockmill C.B. Fairfield County, OH QP open built 1901.

Zeller Smith C.B. Fairfield County, OH closed MKP built 1905.

Stevenson RD C.B. Greene County, OH open Smith built 1877.

Ohio

Scott Town C.B. Lawrence County, OH MKP built 1877.

Boy Scout Camp C.B. Licking County, OH open MKP built unknown, (lovely setting).

Greenway C.B. Licking County, OH closed Town built in 1930 by the CCC.

Ohio

Gregg C.B. Licking County, OH open MKP built 1881.

Eldean C.B. Miami County, OH open Long built 1860 (but passed).

Fletcher C.B. Miami County, OH open Smith built 1998.

Ohio

Foraker C.B. Monroe County, OH open MKP built 1886.

Helmick Mill C.B. Morgan County, OH open MKP built 1867.

Hopewell Church C.B. Perry County, OH open MKP built 1874.

Ohio

Parks/South C.B. Perry County, OH open MKP built 1873.

Roberts C.B. Preble County, OH closed Burr built 1829 (rare two-lane).

Newton Falls (our old) C.B. Trumbull County, OH Town open built 1831.

Ohio

Culbertson C.B. Union County, OH open Partridge built 1868.

Hills C.B. Washington County, OH closed Howe built 1878.

Parker C.B. Wyandot County, OH open Howe built 1873.

Ohio

Brubaker C.B. Preble County, OH open Childs built 1887.

Kirker C.B. Adams County, OH closed MKP built 1867.

Middle Road C.B. Ashtabula County, OH open Howe built 1868.

State Road C.B. Ashtabula County, OH open Town built 1983.

Root Road C.B. Ashtabula County, OH open Town built 1868.

Ohio

South Denmark C.B. Ashtabula County, OH open Town & Arch built 1868.

Riverdale C.B. Ashtabula County, OH open Town built 1874.

Palos C.B. Athens County, OH open MKP built 1875.

Kidwell C.B. Athens County, OH closed Howe built 1800.

Creek Road C.B. Ashtabula County, OH open Town built unknown.

Caine Road C.B. Ashtabula County, OH open Pratt built 1986.

Giddings Road C.B. Ashtabula County, OH open Pratt built 1995.

Ohio

North Pole C.B. Brown County, OH open Smith built 1875.

Bluebird Farm C.B. Carroll County, OH open MKP built 1996.

Charles Harding C.B. Cuyahoga County, OH, MKP built c.1990s (foot traffic only).

George Miller C.B. Brown County, OH open Smith built 1850.

Black C.B. Butler County, OH closed Long built 1870 (rebuilding).

Chambers Road C.B. Delaware County, OH open Childs built 1883.

Hartman C.B. Fairfield County, OH closed QP built 1888 (in Village Park).

Ohio

Mink Hollow C.B. Fairfield County, OH closed MKP built 1887.

Baker C.B. Fairfield County, OH closed MKP built 1871 (on school grounds).

Johnson C.B. Fairfield County, OH closed Howe built 1887 (in park).

Cemetary C.B. Greene County, OH closed Howe built 1886.

Jediah C.B. Hamilton County, OH QP open built 1850.

Johnson Road C.B. Jackson County, OH closed Smith built 1869.

Byer C.B. Jackson County, OH Smith built 1872.

Ohio

Buckeye Furnace C.B. Jackson County, OH open Smith built 1872.

Shoults Girl Scout C.B. Licking County, OH open MKP built 1879 (siding in poor condition).

Davis Farm C.B. Licking County, OH open MKP built 1947.

Bickham C.B. Logan County, OH open Howe built 1877.

Long Knowlton C.B. Monroe County, OH closed MKP & Arch built 1887.

Germantown C.B. Montgomery County, OH closed built 1870 (inverted bowstring).

Ohio

Jasper C.B. Montgomery County, OH closed Arch built 1869.

Adams C.B. Morgan County, OH closed MKP built 1875.

Milton Dye C.B. Morgan County, OH closed MKP built 1915.

Barkhurst C.B. Morgan County, OH open MKP & Arch built 1872.

Parrish C.B. Noble County, OH closed MKP built 1914.

Park Hill/Rich Valley C.B. Noble County, OH closed MKP built unknown (in park), (this was my 400th covered bridge).

Ohio

Huffman Wood C.B. Noble County, OH open MKP built unknown (on private road).

Mary Ruffner C.B. Perry County, OH Smith built 1875 (on private land over pond).

Dixon Branch C.B. Preble County, OH closed Childs built 1887.

Warnke C.B. Preble County, OH open Childs built 1895.

Geeting C.B. Preble County, OH open Childs built 1894.

Christman C.B. Preble County, OH open Childs built 1895.

Harshman C.B. Preble County, OH open Childs built 1894.

Buckskin C.B. Ross County, OH open Smith built 1873.

Ohio

Everett Road C.B. Summitt County, OH closed Smith built 1870.

Upper Darby C.B. Union County, OH open Partridge built 1868.

Bigelow C.B. Union County, OH open Partridge built 1873.

Eakin Mill C.B. Vinton County, OH closed MKP & Arch built unknown (rebuilt 2002).

Greer Mill C.B. Vinton County, OH closed MKP & Arch built 1874.

Cox C.B. Vinton County, OH closed QP built 1884.

Bay C.B. Vinton County, OH closed MKP built 1876.

Mount Olive C.B. Vinton County, OH QP open built 1875.

Ohio

Schwenderman C.B. Washington County, OH closed MKP built 1894 (on private property).

Rinard C.B. Washington County, OH closed Smith built 1876.

Hune C.B. Washington County, OH open Long built 1879.

Root C.B. Washington County, OH closed Long built 1878.

Harra C.B. Washington County C.B. closed Long built 1878 (restored 2002).

Shinn C.B. Washington County, OH closed MKP & Arch built 1886 (being repaired).

Lockport C.B. Williams County, OH open Howe built 1999 (two-lane).

Swartz C.B. Wyandot County, OH open Howe built 1878.

Oregon

Sandy Creek C.B. Coos County, OR, closed, Howe built 1921 (my first covered bridge photo).

Cavitt C.B. Douglas County, OR Howe built 1943.

Antelope Creek, Jackson County, OR QP foot traffic, built 1922.

Oregon

Wimer C.B. Jackson County, OR QP open built 1927.

Currin C.B. Lane County, OR closed Howe built 1925.

Dorena C.B. Lane County, OR open Howe built 1925.

Oregon

Earnest Russell C.B. Lane County, OR open Howe built 1938.

Goodpasture C.B. Lane County, OR Howe built 1938.

Stewart C.B. Lane County, OR closed Howe built 1930.

Oregon

Wildcat C.B. Lane County, OR open, built 1925.

Chitwood C.B. Lincoln County, OR open, Howe built 1930.

Dallenburg/Holley C.B. Linn County, OR Howe built 1989 (was once Weddle foot bridge).

Oregon

Hannah C.B. Linn County, OR open Howe built 1936.

Hoffman C.B. Linn County, OR open Howe built 1936.

Larwood C.B. Linn County, OR open Howe built 1939.

Oregon

Jordan C.B. Marion County, OR closed Sept. 20, 1998 under repair, Howe built 1937.

Hayden C.B. Benton County, OR open Howe built 1918.

Rock O The Range C.B. Deschutes County, OR, KP open built unknown.

Mild Academy C.B. Douglas County, OR open built unknown (heavily reinforced).

Horse Creek C.B. Douglas County, OR closed Howe built unknown.

Oregon

Pass Creek C.B. Douglas County, OR closed for cars Howe built 1925.

Lost Creek C.B. Jackson County, OR QP closed built 1919.

McKee C.B. Jackson County, OR closed Howe built 1917.

Grave Creek C.B. Josephine County, OR open Howe built 1920.

Belknap C.B. Lane County, OR open Howe built 1966.

Coyote Creek C.B. Lane County, OR open Howe built 1922.

Oregon

Lake Creek C.B. Lane County, OR open Howe built 1928.

Deadwood C.B. Lane County, OR open Howe built 1932.

Mosby Creek C.B. Lane County, OR open Howe built 1920.

Centennial walk thru foot C.B. Lane County, OR Howe built 1987.

Lowell C.B. Lane County, OR closed Howe built 1945.

Parvin C.B. Lane County, OR open Howe built 1921.

Pengra C.B. Lane County, OR open Howe built 1928.

Unity C.B. Lane County, OR open Howe built 1936.

Oregon

Mill Creek/Wendling C.B. Lane County, OR open Howe built unknown.

Fisher School C.B. Lincoln County, OR Howe built 1919 (foot traffic only).

Crawfordsville C.B. Linn County, OR closed Howe built 1932.

Short C.B. Linn County, OR open Howe built 1945.

Gilkey C.B. Linn County, OR closed Howe built 1939.

Shimanek C.B. Linn County, OR open Howe built 1966.

Gallon House C.B. Marion County, OR open Howe built 1916.

Cedar Crossing C.B. Multnoma County, OR open built unknown.

Pennsylvania

Heikes Farm C.B. Adams County, PA closed, built 1892.

Claycomb C.B. Bedford County, PA open Burr built 1884.

Diehl/Turner C.B. Bedford County, PA open Burr built 1892.

Pennsylvania

Hewitt C.B. Bedford County, PA open Burr built 1879.

Jackson's Mill C.B. Bedford County, PA open Burr built 1889.

Kutz C.B. Berks County, PA open Burr built 1854.

Pennsylvania

Cabin Run C.B. Bucks County, PA Town open built 1874.

Frankenfield C.B. Bucks County, PA Town open built 1872.

Knechts C.B. Bucks County, PA Town open built 1873.

Pennsylvania

Moods C.B. Bucks County, PA Town open built 1873.

Ralph Stover Park C.B. Bucks County, PA Howe Boxed Pony closed built unknown. Very rare truss.

Twining Ford C.B. Bucks County, PA Town open, destroyed and rebuilt 1997 or 1998.

Pennsylvania

Van Sant C.B. Bucks County, PA Town open built 1875.

Hayes Clark C.B. Chester County, PA QP open built 1871.

Sheeder/Hall C.B. Chester County, PA open Burr built 1850.

Pennsylvania

Speakman No. 2 C.B. Chester County, PA QP open built 1881.

McGees Mill C.B. Clearfield County, PA open Burr built 1873.

Esther Furnace C.B. Columbia County, PA QP open built 1882.

Pennsylvania

Johnson C.B. Columbia County, PA QP open built 1882.

Kramer C.B. Columbia County, PA QP open built 1881.

Ramp C.B. Cumberland County, PA open Burr built 1882.

Pennsylvania

Shade Gap C.B. Huntington County, PA open Howe truss built 1889.

Thomas Ford C.B. Indiana County, PA Town open built 1879.

Colemanville C.B. Lancaster County, PA Burr open, built 1856.

Pennsylvania

Herrs Mill C.B. Lancaster County, PA Burr built 1885.

Kurtz Mill C.B. Lancaster County, PA Burr open built 1876.

Siegrist Mill C.B. Lancaster County, PA Burr open built 1885.

Pennsylvania

Banks C.B. Lawrence County, PA Burr open built 1889.

Schlicher C.B. Lehigh County, PA Burr open built 1882.

Wehr C.B. Lehigh County, PA Burr open built 1841.

Pennsylvania

Mertz C.B. Northumberland County, PA MKP open built 1976.

Rock C.B. Schuykill County, PA Burr open built 1870.

Sam Wagner C.B. Northumberland/Montour County, PA Burr open built 1881.

Pennsylvania

Solts/Kriedersville C.B. Northhampton County, PA Burr closed built 1840.

Klinepeter/Gross C.B. Snyder County, PA Burr open built 1871.

Lower Humbert C.B. Somerset County, PA open Burr built 1891.

Pennsylvania

Pack Saddle C.B. Somerset County, PA open MKP built 1870.

Shaffer C.B. Somerset County, PA Burr open built 1877.

Danley C.B. Washington County, PA open QP built unknown.

Pennsylvania

Day C.B. Washington County, PA open QP built 1875.

Hughes C.B. Washington County, PA closed QP built 1889.

Anderson Farm C.B. Adams County, PA Burr open built unknown.

Jack Mt. C.B. Adams County, PA Burr open built 1892 (traffic light is very rare).

Pennsylvania

Saucks/Sachs C.B. Adams County, PA Town closed built 1864.

Woolslayer C.B. Beaver County, PA closed steel girders built unknown.

Bowser/Osterberg C.B. Bedford County, PA Burr closed built 1890.

Colvin C.B. Bedford County, PA MKP open destroyed and rebuilt in 1990s.

DR Knisley C.B. Bedford County, PA Burr closed built 1867.

Halls Mill C.B. Bedford County, PA Burr open built 1872

Herline C.B. Bedford County, PA Burr open built 1902.

Palo Alto C.B. Bedford County, PA MKP open (private) built 1880.

Pennsylvania

Raystown/Turner C.B. Bedford County, PA Burr open built 1892.

Ryot C.B. Bedford County, PA open built 1868.

Snooks C.B. Bedford County, PA Burr open built 1880.

Dreibelbis C.B. Berks County, PA Burr open built 1869.

Greisemer's Mill C.B. Berks County, PA Burr open built 1832.

Red/Wertz C.B. Berks County, PA Burr closed built 1869.

Erwinna C.B. Bucks County, PA open Town built 1871.

Loux C.B. Bucks County, PA open Town built 1874.

Pennsylvania

Pine Valley C.B. Bucks County, PA Town open built 1842.

Sheards Mill C.B. Bucks County, PA open Town built 1873.

Uhlerstown C.B. Bucks County, PA open Town built 1832.

Bucks/Harrity C.B. Carbon County, PA MKP closed built ca. 1898.

Little Gap C.B. Carbon County, PA Burr open built 1860.

Kennedy C.B. Chester County, PA Burr open built 1856.

Knox/Valley Forge C.B. Chester County, PA Burr open built 1865.

Linton C.B. Chester County, PA Burr open built 1886.

Pennsylvania

Mercers Mill C.B. Chester/Lancaster Counties, PA Burr open built 1860.

Pine Grove C.B. Chester/Lancaster Counties, PA Burr open built 1884.

Rapps Dam C.B. Chester County, PA Burr open built 1866.

Speakman #1 C.B. Chester County, PA Burr open built 1881.

Logan Mill C.B. Clinton County, PA QP open built 1874.

Creasyville C.B. Columbia County, PA QP open built 1881 (my 100th C.B.).

Davis C.B. Columbia County, PA Burr open built 1875 (my 700th covered bridge).

Hollingshead C.B. Columbia County, PA Burr open built 1850.

Pennsylvania

Josiah Hess C.B. Columbia County, PA Burr open built 1875.

Jud Christian C.B. Columbia County, PA QP open built 1876.

Lawrence Knoebel C.B. Columbia County, PA QP open built 1875.

Paar's Mill C.B. Columbia County, PA Burr open built 1865.

Patterson C.B. Columbia County, PA Burr open built 1845.

Richards C.B. Columbia & Northumberland Counties, PA QP open built 1875.

Sam Eckman C.B. Columbia County, PA closed QP built 1876.

Rupert C.B. Columbia County, PA Burr closed built 1847.

Pennsylvania

Shoemaker C.B. Columbia County, PA closed QP built 1881.

Snyder C.B. Columbia County, PA QP open built 1876.

Stillwater C.B. Columbia County, PA Burr closed built 1849.

Wanich C.B. Columbia County, PA Burr open built 1884.

Gudgeonville C.B. Erie County, PA MKP open built c1868.

Bowmansdale C.B. Cumberland/York Counties, PA Burr open built 1867.

West Paden C.B. Columbia County, PA Burr built 1850.

Sherman/Keepville C.B. Erie County, PA MKP open built 1873.

Pennsylvania

Waterford C.B. Erie County, PA Town open built c1875.

Martins Mill C.B. Franklin County, PA closed Town built 1849.

Witherspoon C.B. Franklin County, PA Burr open built 1883.

Cox Farm C.B. Greene County, PA KP open built 1940.

Neddie Woods C.B. Greene County, PA QP open built 1882.

Shriver C.B. Greene County, PA QP open built 1900.

White C.B. Greene County, PA QP open built 1919.

Harmon C.B. Indiana County, PA Town closed built 1910.

Pennsylvania

Kintersberg C.B. Indiana County, PA Howe closed built 1877.

Trusal C.B. Indiana County, PA Town closed built 1870.

McCracken C.B. Jefferson County, PA KP private built 1975.

Academia C.B. Juniata County, PA Burr closed built 1901.

Lehmans C.B. Juniata County, PA open (Stringer) built 1888.

Baumgardners C.B. Lancaster County, PA Burr open built 1860.

Bitzer's Mill C.B. Lancaster County, PA Open Burr built 1846.

Buchers/Cocalico C.B. Lancaster County, PA Burr open built 1892.

Pennsylvania

Buck Hill C.B. Lancaster County, PA Burr closed built 1844 (private).

Erbs/Hammer C.B. Lancaster County, PA Burr open built 1887.

Forry's Mill C.B. Lancaster County, PA Burr open built 1869.

Guy Bard C.B. Lancaster County, PA Burr open built 1891.

Hunseckers Mill C.B. Lancaster County, PA Burr open built 1843.

Jacksons Mill C.B. Lancaster County, PA Burr open built 1878.

Kaufmans C.B. Lancaster County, PA Burr open built 1874.

Landis Mill C.B. Lancaster County, PA MKP open built 1878.

Leamans C.B. Lancaster County, PA Burr open built 1894.

Lime Valley C.B. Lancaster County, PA Burr open built 1871.

Pinetown C.B. Lancaster County, PA Burr open built 1867.

Pools Forge C.B. Lancaster County, PA Burr closed built 1859 (located in cow pasture).

Rissers Mill C.B. Lancaster County, PA Burr open built 1849.

Schenk's Mill C.B. Lancaster County, PA Burr open built 1865.

Shearers Mill C.B. Lancaster County, PA Burr closed built 1856.

Weavers Mill C.B. Lancaster County, PA Burr open built 1879.

Pennsylvania

White Rock Forge C.B. Lancaster County, PA Burr open built 1847.

Willow Hill (Amish) C.B. Lancaster County, PA Burr open built 1962.

Zooks Mill C.B. Lancaster County, PA Burr open built 1849.

McConnell's Mill C.B. Lawrence County, PA open Howe built 1874.

Bogert's C.B. Lehigh County, PA Burr closed built 1841.

Geigers C.B. Lehigh County, PA Burr built 1858.

Manassas Guth C.B. Lehigh County, PA Burr built 1858.

Rex C.B. Lehigh County, PA Burr open built 1858.

Pennsylvania

Buttonwood C.B. Lycoming County, PA MKP & QP open built 1898.

Cogan House C.B. Lycoming County, PA Burr open built 1877.

Lairdsville C.B. Lycoming County, PA Burr open built 1888.

Kidds Mill C.B. Mercer County, PA closed Smith built 1869.

Keefer Mill C.B. Montour County, PA Burr open built 1853.

Keefer Station C.B. Northumberland County, PA Burr open built 1888.

Krickbaum C.B. Northumberland/Columbia Counties, PA QP open built 1876.

Rebuck C.B. Northumberland County, PA MKP open built 1993.

Pennsylvania

Rishel C.B. Northumberland County, PA Burr open built 1830.

Adairs C.B. Perry County, PA Burr open built 1884.

Bistline C.B. Perry County, PA Burr open built 1871.

Books C.B. Perry County, PA Burr closed built 1884.

Clays Wahneta C.B. Perry County, PA Burr open built 1890.

Dellville C.B. Perry County, PA Burr open built 1889.

Enslow C.B. Perry County, PA Burr open built 1904.

Fleishers C.B. Perry County, PA Burr open built 1887.

Pennsylvania

Kochenderfer C.B. Perry County, PA closed Q & KP built 1919.

Mt. Pleasant C.B. Perry County, PA Burr open built 1918.

New Germantown C.B. Perry County, PA open A & KP built 1891.

Rice/Landisburg C.B. Perry County, PA Burr open built 1869.

Saville C.B. Perry County, PA Burr open built 1903.

Wagoners C.B. Perry County, PA Burr closed built 1889.

Zimmermans C.B. Shuykill County, PA Burr open built c1880.

Dreese/Beavertown C.B. Snyder County, PA Burr closed built c1870 (rebuilt 2001).

Pennsylvania

Meiserville C.B. Snyder County, PA Burr closed built 1884 (rebuilt 2001).

North Oriental/Beaver C.B. Snyder/Juniata Counties, PA QP open built 1908.

Barronvale C.B. Somerset County, PA Burr closed built 1902 (this was my 200th covered bridge).

Burkholder C.B. Somerset County, PA Burr open built 1870.

Glessner C.B. Somerset County, PA Burr closed built 1880.

Kings C.B. Somerset County, PA Burr closed built 1906.

Trostletown C.B. Somerset County, PA closed MKP built 1845.

Forksville C.B. Sullivan County, PA Burr open built 1850.

Pennsylvania

Hillsgrove C.B. Sullivan County, PA Burr open built c1850.

Sonestown C.B. Sullivan County, PA Burr open built c1850.

Hassenplug C.B. Union County, PA Burr open built c1825.

Hayes C.B. Union County, PA MKP open built 1882.

Horsham C.B. Union County, PA QP/KP open built 1880.

Brownlee C.B. Washington County, PA KP open built unknown.

Crawford C.B. Washington County, PA QP open built unknown.

Ebenezer C.B. Washington County, PA QP open built unknown.

Pennsylvania

Henry C.B. Washington County, PA QP open built c1881.

Krepps C.B. Washington County, PA KP open built unknown.

Lyle C.B. Washington County, PA QP open built unknown.

Erskine C.B. Washington County, PA QP open built 1845.

Jackson Mill C.B. Washington County, PA QP open built unknown.

Leatherman C.B. Washington County, PA QP open built unknown.

Mays C.B. Washington County, PA QP open built 1882.

Pennsylvania

Pine Bank C.B. Washington County, PA KP park use only built 1870.

Plants C.B. Washington County, PA KP open built 1876.

Sprowls C.B. Washington County, PA KP open built unknown.

Sawhill C.B. Washington County, PA QP open built 1915.

Wilson Mill C.B. Washington County, PA QP open built 1889.

Wright/Cerl C.B. Washington County, PA KP open (destroyed and rebuilt in the 1990s).

South Carolina

Bunker Hill C.B. Catawba County, SC Haupt Truss closed built 1894.

Campbell C.B. Greenville County, SC closed Howe built 1909 (only one in state).

Tennessee

Doe Park C.B. Carter County, TN Smith Truss open built 1882.

Little Chucky C.B. Greene County, TN closed QP built 1922.

Pigeon C.B. Sevier County, TN QP open built 1876.

Vermont

Pulp Mill C.B. Addison County, VT Burr area open built 1820 (another rare two-lane).

Shoreham/Rutland RR C.B. Addison County, VT Howe closed built 1897 (not many of these RR covered bridges left).

Salisbury Station C.B. Addison County, VT open built 1865 (my 600th covered bridge).

Vermont

Chiselville C.B. Bennington County, VT Town open built unknown.

Henry C.B. Bennington County, VT Town open built c1840.

Silk Road C.B. Bennington County, VT Town open built c1840.

Vermont

Chamberlin C.B. Caledonia County, VT QP open built 1881.

Millers Run C.B. Caledonia County, VT Town open built 1878.

Comstock C.B. Franklin County, VT closed lattice built 1883.

Vermont

Longley C.B. Franklin County, VT open lattice built 1863.

Village C.B. Franklin County, VT Burr Arch open built 1867.

Waterville C.B. Lamoille County, VT (Church Street) QP open built unknown.

Vermont

Fisher RR C.B. Lamoille County, VT closed Town lattice built 1908.

Jaynes "Kissing Bridge" C.B. Lamoille County, VT QP open built c1877.

Mill Bridge C.B. Lamoille County, VT open MKP built in 1883 (destroyed by fire after heavy ice damage in winter 1999, has been replaced).

Vermont

Red Bridge C.B. Lamoille County, VT unique open built unknown.

Cilley C.B. Orange County, VT MKP open built 1883.

Flint C.B. Orange County, VT QP open built 1883.

Vermont

Gifford or CK Smith C.B. Orange County, VT open MKP built 1904.

Hyde South Randolph C.B. Orange County, VT open MKP built 1904.

River Road School House C.B. Orleans County, VT lattice troy open built 1885.

Vermont

Moxley C.B. Orange County, VT QP open built 1883.

Brown C.B. Rutland County, VT Town open built 1880.

Cooley C.B. Rutland County, VT Town open built 1849.

Vermont

Lincoln Gap C.B. Washington County, VT lattice open built 1880.

Station C.B. Washington County, VT open lattice built 1872.

Bartonsville C.B. Windham County, VT Town open built 1871.

Vermont

Green River C.B. Windham County, VT Town open built 1873.

Hall C.B. Windham County, VT Town open built 1882.

West Dummerston C.B. Windham County, VT Town open built 1872 (rebuilt 1998).

Vermont

Bowers C.B. Windsor County, VT tied arch open built 1890 (the tied arch truss is rare).

Downers/Upper Falls C.B. (Tour 13) Windsor County, VT MKP open built unknown.

Lincoln C.B. Windsor County, VT Pratt with arch open built 1877.

Vermont

Middle C.B. Windsor County, VT Town open built 1969.

Spade Farm C.B. Addison County, VT Town closed built 1850.

Halpin C.B. Addison County, VT Town open built 1850.

Bridge at the Green C.B. Bennington County, VT Town open built 1852.

Greenbank Hollow C.B. Caledonia County, VT QP open built 1886.

Vermont

School House C.B. Caledonia County, VT QP closed built 1879.

Randall C.B. Caledonia County, VT QP closed built 1865.

Sanborn C.B. Caledonia County, VT Paddleford closed built 1867.

Upper Seguin C.B. Chittendon County, VT Burr Arch open built 1849.

Museum C.B. Chittendon County, VT Burr Arch built 1845 (foot traffic only two-lane).

Lake Shore C.B. Chittendon County, VT tied Arch open built 1898.

Quinlan C.B. Chittendon County, VT Burr Arch open built 1849.

Vermont

Cambridge Junction C.B. Franklin County, VT Burr Arch open built 1887.

Village/Maple St. C.B. Franklin County, VT Town open built 1865.

McMillan C.B. Windham County, VT Stringer closed built 1967 (at Grafton, not on world guide to covered bridge list).

Gold Brook C.B. Lamoille County, VT (Steve Hollow) open Howe built c1900.

Power House C.B. Lamoille County, VT QP open built 1870.

Morgan C.B. Lamoille County, VT QP open built 1887.

Scott Grist Mill C.B. Lamoille County, VT Burr Arch open built 1872.

Vermont

Sayers/Haupt C.B. Orange County, VT Burr Arch open built unknown.

Johnson (Braley) C.B. Orange County, VT MKP open built 1904.

Kingsley C.B. Rutland County, VT Town open built 1836.

Depot C.B. Rutland County, VT Town open built 1853.

Gorham C.B. Rutland County, VT Town open built 1842.

Hammond C.B. Rutland County, VT Town closed built 1843.

Vermont

Coburn C.B. Washington County, VT QP open built 1851.

Pine Brook C.B. Washington County, VT KP open built 1872.

Upper Cox C.B. Washington County, VT QP open built 1872.

Newell C.B. Washington County, VT QP open built 1872.

Union Village C.B. Orange County, VT MKP open built 1867.

Willard C.B. Town open built c1919.

Vermont

Williamsville C.B. Windham County, VT Town open built 1870.

Kidder Hill C.B. Windham County, VT KP open built 1870.

Salmond C.B. Windsor County, VT Town open built 1875.

Quechee C.B. Windsor County, VT Town open built unknown.

Taftsville C.B. Windsor County, VT Burr open built 1836.

Martins Mill C.B. Windsor County, VT Town open built 1881.

Worrall C.B. Windham County, VT Town open built 1868.

Virginia

Humpback C.B. Alleghany County, VA closed Burr built 1857.

Links Farm C.B. Giles County, VA QPV truss built 1912.

Sinking Creek C.B. Giles County, VA closed QP built 1916.

Virginia

Meems C.B. Shenandoah County, VA (near New Market, VA) open Burr built 1892 (this was my 300th bridge to photo).

Jacks Creek C.B. Patrick County, VA QP closed built 1916.

Bob White C.B. Patrick County, QP closed built 1920.

Washington

Grist Mill/Cedar Creek C.B. (near Woodland, WA) Clarke County, WA open built 94/95.

Grays River C.B. Wahkiakum County, WA open Howe built 1905.

SCHAFERS C.B. Grays Harbor County, WA open Howe built 1966.

West Virginia

Phillipi C.B. Barbour County, WV open Burr two-lane built 1852 (only covered bridge in U.S. on U.S. highways 250/119).

Carrollton C.B. Barbour County, WV open Burr built unknown.

Simpson Creek C.B. Harrison County, WV open MKP built 1881.

West Virginia

Herns Mill C.B. Greenbrier County, WV QP open built 1884.

Staats Mill C.B. Jackson County, WV Long truss open built 1888.

Walkersville C.B. Lewis County, WV ("old red") QP open built 1902

West Virginia

Indian Creek C.B. Long Monroe County, WV closed built unknown.

Dents Run C.B. Monogalia County, WV KP open built 1889.

Fletcher C.B. Harrison County, WV open Burr truss built 1891.

West Virginia

Center Point C.B. Doddridge County closed Long built 1888.

Hokes Mill C.B. Greenbriar County, WV near Ronceverte, WV closed Long built 1899 (near collapse).

Sarvis Fork C.B. Jackson County, WV Long & Arch built 1889.

Locust Creek C.B. Pocahontas County, WV closed Warren double intersection (rare) built 1870.

Fish Creek C.B. Wetzel County, WV KP open built 1881.

Wisconsin

Smith Rapids C.B. Price County, WI (near Fifield, WI) Town open built 1991.

Crystal River C.B. Waushara County, WI (near Waupaca, WI), open truss unknown, built unknown.

Springwater C.B. Winnebago County, WI (Saxville, WI) Town open completed in 1997 (average age of construction crew 74 years).

Amnicon C.B. (Suspension Amnicon Falls State Park, WI or Bowstring?) built unknown (foot traffic only).

Cedarburg C.B. Washington County, WI closed town built 1876.

GUIDES AND MAPS

A road atlas is a must. State maps are helpful, especially in VT and NH. These have covered bridge symbols on the road locations. Also Rand McNally Atlases list all states tourism bureaus phone numbers which can be helpful.

County maps; Puetz Place N 2454 Co Rd Lyndon Station WI 53944 Ph 608-666-3331 for current prices etc. They list all counties in the state. The ones for PA have a covered bridge symbol with a line leading to the Co or TWP Rd where the bridge is located. The Ohio maps have a complete listing on all roads and when used in conjunction with the Ohio Historic Bridge Guide you can hardly go wrong. Contact the Ohio Historic Bridge Association for info on getting the guide. There is also a very good covered bridge guide book for IN. Contact Arthur Gatewood Jr., 616 S. Oak St., Fortville, IN 46060-1625 Ph 317-485-5351. There is also a great book for VT. It is divided into 15 tours with roads and covered bridge symbols. contact The New England Press, P.O. Box 575 Shelburne, VT 05482. The author is Joseph C. Nelson. To me it was well worth it. Also by joining the NSPCB you can receive loads of info quarterly. Contact Pauline Prideaux, 143 Freeman St., Ext Haverhill, MA 01830-4659 for membership.

PA Contact Lehigh Valley Visitors Bureau for a self guided tour of Lehigh Co. Ph 1-610-882-9200 or write P.O. Box 20785 Lehigh Valley, PA 18002-0785 also Bedford Co. Visitors Bureau 1-800-765-3331 or write RD, 1 Box 44, Everett PA, 15537 for self guided tour of Bedford Co. PA. Ohio. Ashtabala Co. Covered Bridge Society, 25 West Jefferson St., Jefferson, Ohio 44047 for self guided tour or phone 1-440-576-3769. Indiana Parke Co. Visitors Bureau, P.O. Box 165 Rockville, IN 47872-0165 or phone 1-765-569-5226 for self guided tour information. Once again your road atlas has phone numbers for all states visitors bureaus and some may have additional information besides what is listed here.

COVERED BRIDGES OF THE UNITED STATES

Number	Township	Stream	Name	Spans	Length	Year	Type	Directions
			ALABAMA					
			Blount County					
01-05-05	Cleveland	Locust Fork, Black Warrior River	Swann/Joy	3	320	1933	Town	0.7 SSW jct US231/AL53 on AL79 (south) then 1.0 right on Swann Bridge road.
-07	Horton	Calvert Prong, Little Warrior River	Horton Mill	2	220	1934	Town	5.1 N jct US231 on AL75, then just left on unnamed road. N. Oneonta
-12	Oneonta	Dub Branch, Little Warrior River	Old Easley/ Rosa	1	96	1927	Town	3.4 NW jct AL75 on US231, then 1.5 left on Pine Grobe Rd. at Rosa Church and just left on Old Easley Rd. NW Oneonta
			Calhoun County					
01-08-01	Coldwater	Oxford Lake outflow	Coldwater (closed)	1	64	c1850	King variation	multiple N of Exit 185 of I20 on AL21 then 1st right to Oxford Lake Civic Center. Oxford
			Cullman County					
01-22-01	Clarkson	Crooked Creek	Clarkson/ Legg (closed)	2+	270	1904	Town	7.2 W jct I65 on US278 (Exit 308) then 0.6 right on CR14 and 0.5 left on bypassed section of CR53 in park. (On E side of road)
-12	Berlin (M1958)	Lidy's Lake Outlet	Lidy Walker/Big Branch (permission at Walker's Corner USA/Store) (closed)	1	50	1926	Town	2.7 E jct AL69 on US278, then 0.3 left on CR47 to farm farm access on E side of road.
			DeKalb County					
01-25-02 (formerly -08-03)	Mentone (M1975)	West Fork, Little River	Tallahatchee/ Old Union Crossing (permission)	1	42		MKP	5.0 E jct I59 on AL117 (Exit 231), then 3.0 right to entrance to Cloudmont Ski and Golf Resort, on E side of CR89.
			Etowah County					
01-28-02	Gadsden (M1967)	pond	Gilliland/ Reese City (rebuilt without functional trusses) (closed)	1+	90	1899	Town	1.8 N jct US278/431 to main entrance of Noccalula Falls Park on W side of AL11.
			Lee County					
01-41-04	Salem	Wacoochee Creek	Salem/ Shotwell/ Pea Ridge (closed)	1	76	1900	Town	8.7 SE jct I85 on 3S280/431 (Exit 62), then 1.2 left on CR254 and 0.3 right on CR252.
			Sumter County					
01-60-01	Livingston (M1970)	small lake	Alamuchee/ Bellamy	1+	88	1861	Town	0.6 N jct AL28 on W side of US1 on University of West Alabama campus.
			Talladega County					
01-61-01	Kymulga	Talladega Creek	Kymulga (closed)	1	105	c1860	Howe	1.8 E jct US231/280 on AL76, then 3.8 left on CR180, then 3.7 right on Kymulga Grist Mill Rd. (CR180) and just left on aban- doned road at Kymulga Mill Park NNE Childersburg
-02	Waldo	Talladega Creek	Waldo/ Riddle Mill (closed)	1	115	c1858	Howe and Queen	4.0 SE jct AL21 on AL77 then 0.1 left on private road. At Riddle Mill. SE Talladega

Number	Township	Stream	Name	Spans	Length	Year	Type	Directions
			CALIFORNIA					
			Butte County					
05-04-01	Chico Creek	Butte (closed)	Honey Run	3	230	1896	Pratt and King	1.7 SE jct CA32 on CA99, then 1.4 left on Skyway Rd., 4.4 left on Honey Run Rd., and just right.
-02	Derrick	Oregon Creek	Castleberry (not true truss)	1	35	1984	Warren Bridge	1.5 SW of Feather River on CA70, then 4.5 left on Cherokee Rd., 0.9 left (ahead) on Oregon Gulch Rd., 0.1 left on Derrick Rd.
			Humboldt County					
05-12-02	Rosewood	Elk River	Berta's Ranch	1	52	1936	Queen	0.1 N of Elk River Bridge on US101, then 2.1 right on Elk River Rd., and 0.2 right on Berta's Rd. S Eureka
-05	Rosewood	Elk River	Zane's Ranch	1	52	1937	Queen	0.1 N of Elk River Bridge on US101, then 3.2 right on Elk River Rd., and 0.1 right on Zane's Rd. S Eureka
-08	Bayside	Jacoby Creek	Brookwood	1	66	1969	Howe	2.4 S jct CA299 on US101, exit on Saoma Blvd., 1.9 left on Saoma Blvd./Old Arcata Rd. 1.3 left on Jacoby Creek Rd. and just right. SSE Arcata
			Mariposa County					
05-22-01	Yosemite National Park	South Fork, Merced River	Wawona (admission) (closed)	1	130	1875	Queen	5.5 NNW of south entrance to park on E side of CA441. S. edge on E side of CA441. S. edge Wawona
			Nevada County					
05-29-01	Bridgeport	South Fork, Yuba River	Bridgeport (closed)	1	208	1862	Howe and arch	11.5 NW jct CA20 on CA49, then 6.8 left on Pleasant Valley Rd. and 0.2 right. South Yuba State Park
			Santa Cruz County					
05-44-02	Felton	San Lorenzo River	Felton	1	186	1892	Warren	0.4 E of CA9 on Mt. Hermon Rd., then 0.1 right on Covered Bridge Rd. North on bypassed section of Mt. Hermon Rd.
-03	Paradise Park	San Lorenzo River	Paradise Park (permission) (ask at office)	2	180	1872	Smith	1.0 N jct CA1 on CA9, then 0.8 E. on Keystone Way and just right in Masonic Paradise Park.
-04	Felton	Roaring Creek	Roaring Camp (admission)	1	36	1969	Pratt	0.3 E CA9 and Felton on Mt. Hermon Rd, then 0.7 right to entrance on W side of Graham Hill Rd. Roaring Camp and Big Trees Museum and Railroad
			Stanislaus County					
05-50-01	Oakdale	Stanislaus River	Knight's Ferry (closed)	4	330	1864	Howe	1.0 WSW of Tuolumne County line on CA108/120, then 0.6 right on Old Sonora Rd. S Edge Knight's Ferry
			Yuba County					
05-58-01	Log Cabin	Oregon Creek	Freeman's Crossing/ Oregon Creek	1	105	1882	Queen	0.1 N of Yuba County line on CA49, then 0.2 right on Allegheny Rd. In Tahoe National Forest Day Use Area. N North San Juan

Number	Township	Stream	Name	Spans	Length	Year	Type	Directions
CONNECTICUT								
Hartford County								
07-02-02	Avon	pond outlet	Huckleberry Hill (foot)	1	35	1968	Pratt variation	6.5 W jct I84 on CT4 Exit 39 through Unionville, then 1.7 right on E side of Huckleberry Hill in Avon Countryside Park Rd.
Litchfield County								
07-03-01	Kent	Housatonic River	Bull	1+	109	1842	Town and Queen	3.0 N jct CT39 on US7, then 0.2 left on Bull's Bridge Rd.
-02	Cornwall	Housatonic River	West Cornwall/ Hart	2	242	1841	Town and Queen	Just E of jct US7 on CT128
Middlesex County								
07-04-01	East Comstock	Salmon River	Comstock (closed)	1	80	1873	Howe	2.0 W jct CT149 on CT16, then 0.1 right on bypassed section of CT16. W Westchester
-07	Johnsonville	Moodus River	Johnsonville	1	60	1976	Burr	1.3 W jct CT149 (south) to "T", then 0.8 left on W side of Leesville Rd. (CT609). SW Moodus, at Johnsonville Historical Exhibit.
Tolland County								
07-07-02	Somers	pond	Worthington Pond Farm	1	61	2002	Town	From I84 (exit 70) take CT32 W to CT190. Just before CT83 go right on Mountain Rd. Worthington Pond Farm is on the left
DELAWARE								
New Castle County								
08-02-02	Ashland	Red Clay Creek	Ashland	1	52	c1870	Town	2.0 SE PA State line on DE82 then 0.1 right on Brackenville Rd. ESE Yorklyn
-04	Wooddale	Red Clay Creek	Wooddale (private)	1	60	1870	Town	2.1 ESE jct DE41 on DE48, then 0.3 left on on Rolling Mill Rd, and just left on Foxhill Lane. ESE Hockessin
GEORGIA								
Banks County								
10-06-06	Lula #2	Grove Creek	Lula/ Blind Susie (private)	1	34	1975	King	3.0 E jct GA52 on GA51, then 1.1 right on W side of Antioch Church Rd. Bridge is in woods on right.
Bartow County								
10-08-01	Euharlee	Euharlee Creek	Lowry (closed)	1	138	1886	Town	5.1 WSW jct GA61 on GA113 then 3.0 right through Stilesboro on E (left) side of Covered Bridge Rd.
Cobb County								
10-33-02	Smyrna	Nickajack Creek	Concord/ Ruff Mill/ Nickajack Creek	2+	132	1872	Queen	4.0 N on GA280 from exit 10 of I285, then 2.4 left on Concord Rd.
DeKalb County								
10-44-01 (formerly -29-01)	Stone Mountain (M1957)	Stone Mountain Lake Mountain	College Avenue/Stone Mountain/Effie's (admission) (shortened)	1+	151	1893	Town	1.0 E jct GA236 to main entrance on S side of US78. (ask directions). In Stone Mountain Park

Number	Township	Stream	Name	Spans	Length	Year	Type	Directions
			Early County					
10-49-02	Rock Hill	Coheelee Creek	Coheelee Creek	2	120	1883	modified Queen	0.5 NE jct GA370 on GA62, then 0.6 left on Damascus Hilton Rd., then 1.6 right. (Bridge is on right, next to Fannie Askew Williams Park). NNW Hilton
			Emanuel County					
10-53-M1	Twin City	Fifteen Mile Creek	Parrish Mill (closed) (Mill-Bridge structure)	1+	101	c1888	stringer	4.0 S jct US80 on GA23, then 2.0 left on CR29 (George L. Smith State Park Rd.) to park entrance and 0.3 ahead. In George L. Smith State Park
			Forsyth County					
10-58-01	Heardville	Settendown Creek	Poole's Mill (closed)	1	94	1906	Town	1.1 E of Cherokee County line on GA369, then 0.6 right on Poole's Bridge Park.
-02	Cumming	small creek	Burnt/ Mashburn Estate (permission) (private) (shortened)	1	35	1895	Town	0.1 E jct GA9, then 1.0 left on Pilgrim Mill Rd. (At #515)
			Franklin County					
10-59-01	Cromer's Mills	Nail's Creek	Cromer Mill/ Nail's Creek	1	110	1906	Town	0.6 NE jct GA164 on GA106, then 0.1 right on Cromer Mill Rd. and just Right. WSW Sandy Cross
			Harris County					
10-72-01 formerly -141-02	Pine Mountain	dry land	Wehadkee Creek (admission) (shortened)	1	58	c1870	Town	1.0 S jct GA18 to main entrance. On W side of US27. (bridge is now in storage) At Callaway Gardens
			Madison-Oglethorpe Counties					
10-97-01	Grove Creek Broad	South Fork, Carlton River	Watson Mill/	3	229	c1885	Town	3.0 E jct GA72 on GA22, then 3.2 right on Watson Mill Bridge Rd. In Watson Mill State Park SE Comer
			Meriwether County					
10-99-02	Gay (RB1999)	Big Red Oak Creek	Red Oak Creek/Imlac	1	127	c1840		Town 2.8 N jct GA85 on GA74/85, then 0.1 right on Covered Bridge Rd, then 1.5 left on Brown-Evans Rd.
			Oconee County					
10-108-01	Farmington	Rose Creek	Elder's Mill/ Rose Creek	1	99	1897	Town	5.7 SE jct US129/441 on GA15, then 0.7 right on Elder Mill Rd. SSE Watkinsville
			Oglethorpe County					
10-109-01	Pleasant Hill	Big Clouds Creek	Big Clouds Creek/ Howard	1	162	1905	Town	7.1 N jct US78 on GA22, then 2.2 left on Smithsonia Rd. then 0.1 right on Chandler/Silver Rd. SE Smithsonia
			Upson County					
10-145-02 #2	Hootenville	Auchumpkee Creek	Hootenville/ Auchumpkee Creek	1	120	1997	Town	2.0 NW jct US80 on US19, then 0.7 right on Allen Rd. SSE Thomaston
			White County					
10-154-03	Nacoochee	Chickamauga Creek Chicamauga/ Nacoochee	Stovall Mill/ Helen/Sautee	1	36	1895	Queen	2.7 NNE jct GA17 on S side of highway on bypassed section GA255. NNE Sautee

Number	Township	Stream	Name	Spans	Length	Year	Type	Directions
			ILLINOIS					
			Boone County					
13-04-01	Caledonia	Kinnick Creek Young (foot) (permission	Rockford Bolt Co./	1	75	c1890	Howe	4.0 N jct IL173 on IL76, then 4.7 left on Hunter Rd., then 1.0 left on Harnish Rd. and 0.3 left on Lovesee to farm access on left.
			Bureau County					
13-06-01	Dover	Big Bureau Creek	Red	1	93	1863	Howe	0.7 N jct I80 on IL26 (exit 56), then 0.5 left on old Dixon-Princeton Rd. N Princeton
			Cumberland County					
13-	Greenup	Embarras River	Cumberland	1	200	2002		At Greenup, ask locally.
			Henderson County					
13-36-01	Gladstone	Henderson Creek	Allaman/ Eames (closed)	1	106	1865	Burr	3.4 N jct US34 on E side of IL164, in roadside park.
			Randolph County					
13-79-01	Chester	Little Mary's River	Little Mary's River (closed)	1	98	1854	Burr	4.5 NE jct IL3 on E side of IL150, in roadside park.
			Sangamon County					
13-84-02	Ball	Sugar Creek	Glenarm/ Hedley/ Sugar Creek (closed)	1	58	c1880	multiple King variation and arch	1.2 W of I55 and Glenarm (Exit 83), then 1.0 right and 0.2 right on unnamed road. NW Glenarm
			Shelby County					
13-87-01	Dry Point	Kaskaskia River	Thompson Mill (closed)	1	105	1868	Howe	2.4 W of IL128 and Cowden on CR11, then 0.9 left on W side of bypassed section of unnamed road ENE Cowden
			INDIANA					
			Adams County					
14-01-02	Wabash Channel, Wabash River	Old	Ceylon (closed)	1	135	1862	Howe	1.0 N jct IN116 on US27, then 0.9 right on CR950S (First St), left on Second St, right on High St.
			Bartholomew County					
14-03-04	Columbus (M1986)	Mill Run Creek	New Brownsville	1	96	1840	Long	1.2 ENE jct I65 on IN46 (Exit 68) then left on Brown St. and 0.4 left on 5th St. to Millrace Park entrance and 0.3 ahead
			Brown County					
14-07-01	Jackson	Bean Blossom Creek	Bean Blossom Creek	1	69	1880	Howe variation	Just S jct IN45 on IN135, then 0.7 right on Covered Bridge Rd.
-02	Washington (M1932)	Salt Creek	Ramp Creek	1	110	1838	Burr	1.7 E jct IN46/135 and Nashville on combined routes, then 0.1 right at N entrance to Brown County State Park. ESE Nashville
			Carroll County					
14-08-01	Democrat	North Fork, Wildcat Creek	Adams Mill (closed)	1	149	1872	Howe and arch	0.5 N of IN75 on Meridan Rd. to Cutler, then 0.8 right on CR500S and 0.5 Left on CR75. NE Cutler
-02	Clay	North Fork, Wildcat Creek	Lancaster/ Beard	1	134	1872	Howe	0.6 E of US421/IN39 and Owasco on CR600S, then 0.5 left on CR500W. E Owasco

Number	Township	Stream	Name	Spans	Length	Year	Type	Directions
			Dearborn County					
14-15-01 #2	Miller (M1960)	unnamed gully	Guilford	1	119	1879	Burr variation	0.8 W of I275 (exit 16) US50, then 0.3 ahead on unmarked road, 5.4 right on IN1 and just left in a roadside park E edge Guilford
			Decatur County					
14-16-01	Sand Creek	Sand Creek	Westport (closed)	1	131	1880	Burr	2.2 E of IN3 and traffic signal on W Main St. (CR1100S) then 0.1 left on bypassed section of CR1100S. SE edge Westport
			DeKalb County					
14-17-01	Spencer	St. Joseph River	Coburn/ Spencerville	1+	160	1873	Smith (#4)	1.3 N of Allen County line on IN1, then 0.3 right on Front St. E edge Spencerville
			Fayette County					
14-21-01	Connersville (M1984)	dry land	Longwood (closed)	1	104	1884	Burr	In Connersville at IN1 North and 28th St. in Roberts Park.
			Fountain County					
14-23-01	Jackson	Sugar Mill Creek	Wallace (closed)	1	81	1871	Howe	1.0 N jct IN234 on IN341, 0.3 right on Lutheran Church Rd. and just left on bypassed section of CR1000S. E edge Wallace
-02	Wabash	Coal Creek	Cade Mill (closed	1	159	1854	Howe	3.6 W jct US41 on IN32, then 1.0 right and 1.0 left on Glasscock Rd. and 0.3 left on W. Cade's Hollow Rd. SW Weedersburg
-03	Shawnee	Big Shawnee Creek	Rob Roy	1	120	1860	Howe	0.5 N jct IN55 on US41, then 0.2 left on Covered Bridge Rd N edge Rob Roy
			Franklin County					
14-24-05	Ray	Salt Creek	Stock- heughter/ Enochsburg	1	101	1887	Howe	0.3 S of I74 to New Point (Exit 143), then 1.7 left on IN46, 1.8 left on County Line Rd (CR1475E) and 0.8 right on Enochsburg Rd (CR1480W). E Enochsburg
-09	Whitewater	Johnson Fork, Whitewater River	Snow Hill	1	83	1894	Howe	1.1 W jct I74 on US52 (Exit 169 then 3.7 left on Johnson Fork Rd (CR800E), and just left on Snow Hill Rd(CR660S). N Rockdale
-10	Springfield	Big Cedar Creek	Seal/Barn (permission) (private)	1	54	1905	Queen	6.0 E of jct IN1/US52 on IN252, then 0.6 right on Big Cedar Rd. (CR620E) W Mt. Carmel
-11	Metamora	Duck Creek	Canal Aqueduct	1	82	1846	Burr	1.0 E jct IN229 on US52, then 0.1 right at sign for Whitewater Canal State Historical Site and 0.2 left on N side of Main St.
			Gibson County					
14-26-01	Wabash	Big Bayou Creek	Old Red (closed)	1+	178	1875	Smith	1.7 N of Posey County line on IN165, then 0.7 left on CR875S, 0.1 right on CR1250W, 4.3 left on CR850S, 2.0 on CR1675W (CR1660W) CR1675W. SW Crawleyville

Number	Township	Stream	Name	Spans	Length	Year	Type	Directions
			(cont'd) Gibson County					
-03	Washington	Patoka River	Wheeling (closed)	1	168	1877	Smith	From Princeton take IN65 to CR400N, then 3.7 right On bypassed section of CR375N, On S side of road. NE Princeton
			Grant County					
14-27-01	Jefferson	Mississi-newa River	Cumberland/ Matthews	1	181	1877	Howe	1.0 S IN26 on CR950E, then 0.5 left on CR1000S, then 1.4 right on C1000E SE edge Matthews
			Greene County					
14-28-01	Taylor	Richland Creek	Richland Creek (closed)	1	100	1883	Burr	Go W from Bloomfield on combined US231/IN54 to Seminary Rd. and 2.4 right. S Bloomfield
			Hamilton County					
14-29-01	Noblesville	West Fork, White River	Potter (closed)	2	259	1871	Howe	0.1 W jct IN37 on IN32/38, then 1.8 right on Cumberland Rd and 0.3 left on Allisonville Rd.
-02 formerly -17-01	Delaware	ravine	Cedar Chapel (closed) (private)	1	118	1884	Howe	0.2 S of main entrance to Conner Prairie Museum and Pioneer Settlement, on W side of Allisonville Request permission at Museum. Noblesville
			Howard County					
14-34-01	Kokomo (M1958)	Kokomo Creek	Vermont (closed)	1	111	1875	Smith	0.4 S jct US35/IN22 on Business US31 (S. Washington St), then 0.6 right on Deffenbaugh St to entrance to Highland Park and just ahead.
			Jackson County					
14-36-02	Brownstown-Hamilton	East Fork, White River	Shieldstown (closed)	2	353	1876	Burr	3.3 NE jct IN39 on US50, then 1.0 left on Crane/Shield Rd., just before the tall water tower NE Brownstown
-03	Hamilton-Jackson	East Fork, White River	Bell's Ford (closed) (only 1 span Remains)	2	330	1869	Post	2.7 WNW jct IN11, and IN258 on bypassed section of IN258 on N side of highway. WNW Seymour
-04	Carr-Driftwood	East Fork, White River	Medora (closed)	3	459	1875	Burr	2.3 W jct IN135 on bypassed section of IN235 on N side of highway. E Medora
			Jennings County					
14-40-01	Geneva	Sand Creek	Scipio	1	156	1886	Howe	8.0 NW US50 on IN7 then 0.3 right on CR575W. N edge Scipio
-02	Lovette	Big Graham	James Creek	1	139	1887	Howe	6.0 S jct IN7 on IN3, then 0.6 left on CR650S.
			Lake County					
14-45-01	Center (M1933)	dry land Shelhurn	Milroy/ Crown Point/ Fairgrounds	1	85	1878	Burr	1.3 N on US321 from exit 247 of I65 to Greenwood Ave in Crown Point, then 1.4 left to County Fairgrounds. 0.3 S on Court St. to entrance W edge Crown Point

Number	Township	Stream	Name	Spans	Length	Year	Type	Directions
Lawrence County								
14-47-02	Spice Vallley	East Fork, White River	Williams	2	347	1884	Howe	1.3 E of Martin County line on IN450, then 0.4 right on CR1000W. W Williams
Marion County								
14-49-01	Pike (M1960)	Branch of Fishback Creek	Traders Point/ D.W. Brown (closed) (private)	1	88	1880	Howe	0.7 W of Lafayette Rd (old US52) ot 9123 West 86th St. (No admittance, reference only)
Montgomery County								
14-54-01	Franklin	Sugar Creek	Darlington	2	169	1868	Howe	0.4 N of IN47 on CR625E. then 0.3 right on Main St. (CR500N).and 0.2 left on bypassed section of CR500N. W edge Darlington
-03	Brown-Ripley	Sugar Creek	Deer's Mill (closed)	2	275	1878	Burr	6.6 WNW jct IN47 or 6.5 ESE jct IN341 on W side of highway on bypassed section of IN234 on E edge of Shades State Park
Owen County								
14-60-01	Jennings	Mill Creek (admission)	Cataract Falls (closed)	1	140	1876	Smith	2.3 S Putnam County line on US231, then 3.2 right at sign for Cataract Falls Recreation Area and just right on bypassed section of CR75N. NE Cataract
Parke County								
14-61-01 PC6	Jackson	Big Rocky Fork Creek	Big Rocky Fork/Murphy (closed)	1	88	1900	Burr	0.9 S of Big Racoon Creek Bridge on IN59, then 1.4 left Rocky Fork Rd. SE Mansfield
-02 PC7	Raccoon	Big Raccoon Creek	Conley's Ford	1	211	1907	Burr	0.9 S of Big Raccoon Creek Bridge on IN59, 1.4 right on CR720S and 0.3 right. WSW Mansfield
-03 PC9	Raccoon	Big Raccoon Creek	Jeffries Ford	2	222	1915	Burr	2.4 SSW of Bridgeton on CR320E, then 0.5 left on CR150E. SW Bridgeton
-04 PC8	Raccoon	Big Raccoon Creek	Bridgeton (closed)	2	267	1868	Burr	0.1 N of CR320E on W side of road on bypassed section of CR780S. N edge Bridgeton
-05 PC14	Raccoon	Little Raccoon Creek	Nevins	1	168	1920	Burr	1.2 E of CR40E and Catlin on CR500S, then 0.6 right on CR170E. ESE Catlin
-07 PC16	Florida	Big Raccoon Creek	Thorpe Ford (closed)	1	181	1912	Burr	0.3 E on Central Rd. from Rosedale then left on Cemetary Rd. (CR200W) which becomes CR40E. NE Rosedale
-09 PC18	Florida	Big Raccoon Creek	Roseville/ Coxville	2	280	1910	Burr	2.2 NNW of CR100S and Rosedale on CR550W, then 0.1 right on CR25W. At Coxville
-10 PC19	Florida	Rock Run Creek	Harry Evans	1	80	1908	Burr	0.4 NNE of CR550W and Coxville on CR225W, then 0.6 left on CR225W. NNW Coxville

Number	Township	Stream	Name	Spans	Length	Year	Type	Directions
			(cont'd) Parke County, Indiana					
-11 PC20	Florida	Rock Run Creek	Zacke Cox	1	70	1908	Burr	0.4 NNE of CR550W and Coxville on CR225W, then 3.2 left on CR325W, and 0.4 right on CR500S. N Coxville
-12 PC22	Wabash	Big Pond Creek	Phillips	1	60	1909	multiple King	2.5 E of Montezuma on US36 then 0.7 right on CR310W and 0.1 right on CR450W. SE Montezuma
-13 PC21	Wabash	Big Raccoon Creek	Mecca (closed)	1	178	1873	Burr	1.4 N of US41 on CR550W, then 0.3 right on S side of road on bypassed section of CR275S. of W edge Mecca
-14 PC23	Wabash	Leatherwood Creek	Sim Smith/ Leatherwood Ford	1	101	1883	Burr	2.5 E of Montezuma on US36, then 0.2 right on CR310W/ (old US36). SE Montezuma
-15 PC13	Adams (M1961)	Bill Diddle Creek	Catlin (closed)	1	70	1907	Burr	1.6 N jct US36 on W side of US41 on County golf course.
-16 PC11	Adams	Little Raccoon Creek	McAllister	1	142	1914	Burr	1.2 W of CR640E and Catlin on CR500S, then 0.8 left on CR130E, 0.3 right and 0.8 right on CR400S.
-17 PC12	Adams (RB1967)	Little Raccoon Creek	NE Catlin Crooks	1	153	1855	Burr	0.2 E jct US41 on US36, 1.5 right on CR80. When road turns left, go straight on dirt road. SE Rockville
-18 PC15	Adams	Little Raccoon Creek	Neet (bypassed)	1	151	1904	Burr	E of CR40E on CR500S, left on CR170E, right on 400S, then left on CR200E. ENE Catlin
-19 PC39	Adams	Williams Creek	Billie Creek (admission)	1	77	1895	Burr	1.4 E jct US41 on US36 to Billie Creek Village. E Rockville
-20 PC5	Jackson	Big Raccoon Creek	Mansfield	2	275	1867	Burr	In center of Mansfield, next to Mansfield Mall. Mansfield
-21 PC34	Greene (M1961)	Little Raccoon Creek	Portland Mills/ Dooley Station (closed) (arson damage 1989)	1	130	1856	Burr	0.2 E jct IN59 (south)/IN236 (west) on combined routes, then 1.0 left on CR720E and 0.1 right on CR650N. NE Guion
-24 PC38	Adams (M1981)	dry land	Beeson (closed) (admission)	1	55	1906	Burr	Same as -61-19. In Billie Creek Village.
-25 PC25	Adams	Williams Creek	Leatherwood (closed) (admission)	1	72	1899	Burr	Same as -61-19. In Billie Creek Village.
-26 PC24	Reserve	Leather- wood Creek	Melcher/ Klondyke/ Marion	1	83	1896	Burr	1.0 E of Montezuma on US36. then 1.2 left on CR20N. E Montezuma
-27 PC26	Reserve	Sugar Creek	West Union (closed)	2	315	1876	Burr	0.5 N of West Union on E side of bypassed section of CR525W. West Union

Number	Township	Stream	Name	Spans	Length	Year	Type	Directions
			(cont'd) Parke County					
-28 PC28	Penn	Sugar Creek	Jackson/ Rockport Wright's Mill	1	207	1861	Burr	Go 1.4 S from CR1050N in Sylvania on CR425W and 0.3 left and 1.4 right on CR250W. Annapolis
-29 PC31	Liberty	Mill Creek	Mill Creek/ Earl Ray/ Thompson's Ford	1	92	1907	Burr	0.8 W of CR700W and Howard on CR1050N, then 0.4 right on CR550W.
-31 PC30	Liberty	Rush Creek	Rush Creek	1	95	1904	Burr	Go S of Tangier on CR425W, then 0.6 left on CR900N.
-32 PC29	Liberty	Rush Creek	Marshall	1	72	1917	Burr	0.3 W of CR400W and Tangier on CR1050N, then 2.6 left on CR450W and 0.2 left on CR800N.
-33 PC32	Liberty	Mill Creek	Bowsher Ford	1	981	1915	Burr	0.8 E of CR700W and Howard on CR1050N, then 1.2 left on CR550W and 0.2 right on CR1125N
-34 PC36	Penn	Sugar Creek	Cox Ford	1	192	1913	Burr	0.7 W jct US41 on IN47, then 0.7 left on CR110E. In Turkey Run State Park. Marshall
-35 PC35	Sugar Creek	Sugar Creek	Wilkins Mill	1	120	1906	Burr	0.9 N jct IN47 on US41, then 0.2 right in CR850N. NW Marshall
-36 PC37	Sugar Creek	Sugar Creek	Narrows (closed)	1	141	1882	Burr	0.8 E of main entrance to Turkey Run State Park on IN47, then 0.7 left on W side of CR300E
-38 PC1	Adams	Little Raccoon (private)	State Sanatorium Creek (closed)	1	168	1910	Burr	3.1 E jct US41 on US36, then 0.8 left on CR350E and 0.2 right on abandoned Road.
			Perry-Spencer Counties					
14-62-01 -74-01	Anderson- Harrison	Anderson River	Huffman Mill	1	158	1884	Burr	6.0 N jct IN66 on IN545, 3.0 right or 10.7 N jct IN37 on IN545, then 4.7 left and 0.2 left on CR1490N. N edge Huffman
			Putnam County					
14-67-01	Franklin	Cornstalk River	Cornstalk	1	97	1917	Burr	0.4 N jct IN236 on US231, then 0.1 right to Raccoon, 0.1 right on old Rte. 231 and 1.9 left ENE Raccoon
-02	Floyd	Big Walnut Creek	Hillis/ Baker Camp	1	147	c1905	Burr	1.0 E of Washington St. traffic signal on US36, then 1.6 right on CR300S. ESE Bainbridge
-03	Jackson	Big Walnut Creek	Pine Bluff	2	217		Howe	1.5 NNE of US36 and traffic signal on N Washington St then 2.0 right on CR950N. NE Bainbridge

Number	Township	Stream	Name	Spans	Length	Year	Type	Directions
			(cont'd) Putnam County					
-04	Floyd	Big Walnut Creek	Rollingstone	1	116	1915	Burr	1.4 N of US36 and traffic signal on N Washington St (CR200E), then 1.2 right (ahead) on CR800N. ENE Bainbridge
-06	Clinton	Little Walnut Creek	Edna Collins	1	94	1922	Burr	From IN36, W of US231 go 3.5 S on CR600W, 0.2 right on CR350N and 1.1 straight on CR625W to CR450N, then 0.1 left. NW Clinton Falls
-07	Madison	Big Walnut Creek	Dunbar	2	198	1880	Burr	Take US231 N from Greencastle, then 0.4 left on on CR25S, after railroad arch bridge, and 0.6 right on CR125W. NW Greencastle
-10	Madison	Big Walnut Creek	Oakalla/ Shoppell	1	180	1898	Burr	2.0 SSW of US231 and Courthouse on Jackson St/ Manhattan Rd to Limedale, then 2.1 right on CR300S and 0.5 right on CR375W. SW Greencastle
-11	Washington	Big Walnut Creek	Houck	2	212	1884	Howe	Take US40 to Manhattan, 2.0 left on CR445W Manhattan-Greencastle Rd, then 1.2 left on CR550S NNW Manhattan
-13	Washington	Big Walnut Creek	Webster/ Dick Huffman	2	268	1880	Howe	Go 2.3 S on CR625W from US40 inPleasant Gardens, 1.0 right on CR550W (becomes CR525W) and and 0.2 right on CR1050S.
			Ripley County					
14-69-02	Otter Creek	Otter Creek	Holton/ Otter Creek	1	112	1884	Howe	5.0 W jct US421 on US50, then 1.0 right (ahead) through Holton and 1.2 right on CR850W. WNW Holton
-04	Johnson Creek	Laughery	Busching	1	176	1885	Howe	1.1 ESE jct US421 and US50, then 0.6 left and just left at W edge of Versailles State Park. E Versailles
			Rush County					
14-70-01	Rushville	Big Flat Rock River	Smith/ Ewbank	1	124	1877	Burr	0.1 N jct IN44 on IN3, then 0.2 right on 3rd St, 2.0 left on Fort Wayne Ave CR100E and 0.4 right on CR150N. NE Rushville
-02	Posey	Little Blue River	Offutt's Ford (closed)	1	100	1884	Burr	0.9 N of US52 and Arlington on CR700 W, then 2.3 right on CR300N and 0.5 left on Offutt Ford Rd. NE Arlington
-04	Orange	Flat Rock River	Forsythe Mill	1	197	1888	Burr	3.2 W jct IN3 on IN44, then 1.6 right on CR500W and just left on CR650S. WNW Milroy
-07	Orange	Flat Rock River	Moscow	2	335	1886	Burr	1.1 S of IN244 on CR640W to Moscow, then just left on CR650S. At Moscow

Number	Township	Stream	Name	Spans	Length	Year	Type	Directions
			(cont'd) **Rush County**					
-08	Jackson	Flat Rock River	Norris Ford	1	169	1916	Burr	0.2 right on 3rd St, 3.6 left on Fort Wayne Ave. (CR100E/125E), and 0.5 right on CR100N. NNE Rushville
-18	Walker	dry land	Homer/Barn (permission) (private)	1	53	1881 King	multiple	Go 0.2 S from CR715W in Homer to CR250S. Go 0.2 right and walk 0.1 S. S edge Homer
			Shelby County					
14-73-01	Addison (M1975)	dry land	Cedar Ford	1	143	1885	Burr	Removed to Ohio in 1996.
			Vermillion County					
14-83-02	Clinton (M1994)	Brouillett's Creek	S. Hill (closed)	1	122	1879	Burr	Dismantled and in storage at Geneva Hills Golf Course.
-03	Helt	dry land	Hillsdale (closed)	1	125	1876	Burr	1.8 E jct IN71 on N side of US36 in Ernie Pyle Park. SE Dana
-04	Newport	Little Vermillion River	Newport (closed)	1	205	1885	Burr	0.8 S jct IN63 on IN71, then 0.6 left on CR150E. (at cemetery), then 0.5 left on CR75N.
-05	Eugene	Vermillion River	Eugene (closed)	1	212	1885	Burr	1.0 W jct IN63 on IN234, then 1.0 right on Elm Tree Rd and 0.2 left on CR100W.
			Vigo County					
14-84-02	Linton	pond	Irishman (closed)	1	84	c1847	Queen	Take IN154 S from Riley and go 0.1 right on Oregon Church Rd to Fowler Park. SSW Terre Haute
			Wabash County					
14-85-01	Paw Paw (RB1992)	Eel River	Roann	2	300	1872	Howe	1.8 W jct IN15 on IN16, then 0.3 right on Old Chippewa Rd. N edge Roann
-02	Chester	Eel River	North Manchester	1	150	1872	Smith	1.2 E jct IN13 onIN114 (Main St), then 0.2 right on on Sycamore St. SE Section North Manchester

IOWA
Keokuk County

Number	Township	Stream	Name	Spans	Length	Year	Type	Directions
15-54-01	Warren	North Skunk River	Delta (closed)	1	76	1969	Burr	5.0 S jct IA92 on IA21, then 0.5 left on Old Mill Rd and 0.2 left at Kensler Cemetery. S Delta
			Madison County					
15-61-02	Union (M1970)	ditch	Cutler Donahue (closed)	1	79	1871	Town	0.8 S jct IA169/IA92 on Business Rte 169, then 0.8 left on E Court Ave and 0.3 right on 9th St to City Park entrance. SSE Winterset
-03	Union	Cedar Creek	Cedar/ Casper	1	76	1883	Town	0.5 E jct US169 on IA92 then 1.5 left, 0.2 right and 0.1 left
-04	Douglas	North	Hogback	1	106	1884	Town	3.8 N jct IA92 on IA/US169, then 2.6 left, 0.2 left and 0.8 ahead. NNW Winterset

Number	Township	Stream	Name	Spans	Length	Year	Type	Directions
			(cont'd) Madison County					
-05	Scott	Middle River	Holliwell (closed)	1	122	1880	Town and arch	1.5 W jct US169 on IA92, then 1.0 right and 1.7 left on Scott Township Rd. ESE Winterset
-06	South (M1977)	brook	Imes/King (closed)	1	81	1870	Town	0.5 W of I35 on CR G50 (Exit 52) (bridge is on S side of road in Imes Bridge Park) E edge St.Charles
-07	Webster	Middle River	Roseman/ Oak Grove (closed)	1	107	1883	Town and Queen	7.3 W jct US169 on IA92, then 1.9 left, 1.3 left, and just left on Webster Township Rd. WSW Winterset
			Marion County					
15-63-01	Indiana	North Cedar Creek	Hammond	1	80	1870	Howe	2.0 S of IA5 and Attica on CR G76, then 0.2 left and 2.0 right on Indiana Township Rd. S Attica
-04 formerly 1/2 of-63-02	Liberty (M1971)	ravine	Wilcox Game Preserve/ Marysville (closed)	1	40	1891	Town	2.5 E of CR G76 and Attica on IA5, then 1.5 N on T17, then 0.2 S. ENE Attica
-05 formerly 1/2 of -63-02	Knoxville (M1968)	ravine	Marysville (closed)	1	41	1891	Town	0.1 N jct IA92 BP on IA14, then 0.5 left on Willetts Dr. and 0.2 left at Marion County Park entrance (take right fork, bridge is on S side of road.)
			Polk County					
15-77-01	Allen	arm of Yeader Creek	Owens (closed)	1	100	1888	Howe	1.5 E jct US65/69 on IA5, then 1.0 left on Indianola Ave.,1.0 right on Easter Lake Dr and 0.5 left in Easter Lake Park (E of Ewing Park). SE Des Moines
			KENTUCKY *Bourbon County*					
17-09-03	Ruddel's Mills	Hinkston Creek	Colville Pike	1	120	1877	multiple King	3.0 WNW of US68 and S edge of Millersburg on KY1893, then 1.0 right on Colville Rd. NW Millersburg
			Bracken County					
17-12-01	Wellsburg	Locust Creek	Walcott/ White (closed)	1	73	c1880	multiple King and Queen	1.0 N jct KY8 at jct with KY546 on bypassed section of KY1159. NNW Brooksville
			Fleming County					
17-35-04	Flemingburg (M1984)	Fox Creek	Ringo Mill (closed)	1	88	1867	multiple King	3.7 SE jct KY111 on E side of highway on bypassed section of KY158. SE Hillsboro
-05	Grange City	Fox Creek	Grange City/ Hillsboro (closed)	1	86	c1867	multiple King	3.0 S jct KY158 on W side of highway on bypassed section of KY111. S Hillsboro
-06	Goddard	Sandlick Creek White	Goddard/	1	63		Town	4.8 SE jct KY111 on KY32, then just left on Maddox Rd.

Number	Township	Stream	Name	Spans	Length	Year	Type	Directions
			Franklin County					
17-37-01	Switzer (RB1997)	North Elkhorn Creek	Switzer (closed) (washed away)	1	120	1855	Howe	4.1 E jct US60 on US460, then 3.6 left on E side of bypassed section of KY22.
			Greenup County					
17-45-01	Lynn	Tygart's Creek	Bennett Mill	1	155	1875	Wheeler	8.2 SSE jct US23 on KY7, 0.1 left on Tygart's Creek Rd. (KY1215). SSE South Shore
-02	Oldtown	Little Sandy Creek	Oldtown (closed)	2	188	1870	multiple King	1.7 N jct KY784 on KY 1, then just right on Frazer Rd. (CR705). N Hopewell
			Lewis County					
17-68-03	Rectorville	Cabin Creek	Cabin Creek/ Mackey-Hughes Farm (closed)	1	114	1867	multiple King	6.7 W jct KY57 on S side of highway. Go 2.0 to fork, then 1.6 left on bypassed section of KY984. NW Tollesboro
			Mason County					
17-81-01	Dover	Lee's Creek	Dover	1+	63	c1835	Queen variation	0.4 E of KY135 and Dover on KY8, then 0.1 right on Lee's Creek Rd (SR3113).
-02	Fernleaf	Lee's Creek tributary (private)	Valley Pike/ Bouldin	1	24	1864	King	0.8 E jct KY10 on KY435, then 1.5 left on Valley Pike at No. 421. ENE Germantown
			Robertson County					
17-101-01	Blue Lick Springs	Johnson Creek	Johnson Creek (closed)	1+	112	1874	Smith (2)	1.6 N jct US68 on KY165, then 2.2 right on bypassed section of Blue Licks Rd (KY1029).
			Washington County					
17-115-01	Mooresville	Beech Fork River	Beech Fork/ Mooresvile (closed)	2	211	1865	Burr	5.7 S jct US62 or 2.4 N jct KY55 on W side of bypassed section of KY458. S Chaplin

MAINE
Aroostook County

Number	Township	Stream	Name	Spans	Length	Year	Type	Directions
19-02-01	Littleton	Meduxnekeag River (closed)	Watson Settlement	2	160	1903	Howe	1.6 E of US1 and Littleton-Ingraham Rd, then 1.5 right on Framingham Rd, and 0.3 left on bypassed section of Carson Rd.
			Cumberland County					
19-03-01 #2	Gorham-Windham	Presumpscot River	Babb's	1	79	1976	Queen	1.1 N jct ME237 on US202/ME4, then 1.6 left on River Rd and 0.4 left on Hurricane Rd. NNW South Windham
			Oxford County					
19-09-01	Andover	Ellis River	Lovejoy	1	80	1867	Paddleford	3.2 S jct ME120 and Andover on ME 5, then 0.2 left on unnamed road. E edge South Andover
19-09-02	Fryeburg	Old Channel Saco River	Hemlock	1	116	1857	Paddleford and arch	6.0 E jct ME5 and Fryeburg on US302, then 3.0 left on Hemlock Bridge Rd. (seasonal access) NNW East Fryeburg

Number	Township	Stream	Name	Spans	Length	Year	Type	Directions
	*(cont'd) Oxford County*							
-03	Lincoln Plantation	Magalloway River	Bennett (closed)	1	100	1901	Paddleford	1.5 S of Wilson's Mills on ME16, then 0.4 right on bypassed section of unnamed road. S Wilson's Mills
-04	Newry	Sunday River	Sunday River/Artist	1	100	1870	Paddleford	2.7 N jct ME5/26 and Bethel on US2/ME5/26. then 3.7 left on bypassed section of Sunday River Rd. NW North Bethel
	*Oxford York Counties*							
19-09-05 -16-01	Parsonfield-Porter	Ossippee River	Porter/ Parsonfield	2	160	1858	Paddleford	0.3 S jct ME25 and Porter on E side of bypassed section of ME160. S Porter
	*Penobscot County*							
19-10-02	Corinth	Kenduskeag Stream	Robyville	1	76	1876	Long	1.2 N on ME15 from main instersection in Kenduskeag, 1.3 left on Cushman Rd, then 0.2 and just left on Robyville Rd. NNW Kenduskeag
-23	Bradley	Blackman's Stream	Conard's Mill	1	52	1989	Town	4.5 N of ME9, 1.2 E of ME178 on Government Rd. S Bradley Village
-24	Bangor	unnamed stream	Cole Land Transportation Museum	1	72	1994	Howe	405 Perry Rd at exit 45A of I95 and I395.
	*Piscataquis County*							
19-11-01 #2	Guilford-Sangerville	Piscataquis River	Lowe's	1	130	1990	Long	2.3 right jct ME23 on ME6/15/16 then 0.1 right on unnamed road. ENE Sangerville
	*Somerset County*							
19-13-S1	New Portland	Carrabassett River	Wire	1	198	c1868	covered wooden tower suspension	0.1 E jct ME27 on ME146, then 0.1 left and 0.7 right on Wire Bridge Rd. NE New Portland
	*York County*							
19-16-P1	South Berwick	Boston & Maine	Hobbs	1	40		boxed pony Railroad	3.0 NNE jct ME236 on ME4, then just left on old Rte 4. NE South Berwick

MARYLAND
Baltimore-Harford Counties

Number	Township	Stream	Name	Spans	Length	Year	Type	Directions
20-03-02	North Franklinville	Little Gunpowder Falls	Jericho	1	88	1858	Burr	1.8 NE of US1 and Kingsville on Jerusalem Rd, then 0.3 right on Jericho Rd. ENE Kingsville
	*Cecil County*							
20-07-01	Bay View (RB1959)	Northeast Creek	Gilpin	1	119	1860	Burr	1.2 N jct I95 on E side of bypassed section of MD272. (Exit 8) NE Bayview
-02	Fair Hill (RB1992)	Big Elk Creek (private) (permission)	Foxcatcher Farm	1	80	c1860	Burr	0.3 N of MD273 on MD213 and right into Fairhill Training Center. Go 1.7, then 1.1 left on Tawes Dr.

Number	Township	Stream	Name	Spans	Length	Year	Type	Directions
Frederick County								
20-10-01	Lewistown (M1987) (RB1997)	Fishing	Utica Mills	2	100	c1850	Burr	0.2 S of main intersection in Lewistown on MD806, then 0.9 left on Utica Rd.
-02	Thurmont	Owens	Roddy (RB1996)	1 Creek	39	c1850	King	1.0 E jct US15, on MD77, then 0.8 left on Apples Church Rd and 0.8 ahead on Roddy Rd.
-03	Creagerstown (RB1994)	Owens Creek	Loy's	2	90	1994	multiple King	0.2 N of main instersection in Creagerstown on MD550.

MASSACHUSETTS
Berkshire County

Number	Township	Stream	Name	Spans	Length	Year	Type	Directions
21-02-01 #2	Sheffield	Housatonic River	Upper Sheffield	1	93	1998	Town	0.8 N of main intersection in Sheffield on US7, then 0.2 right on Covered Bridge Lane. Opposite Cook Road.
Essex County								
21-05-01	Gloucester	Sawyer Pond	Sawyer Pond	1	43	1990	Town	1.1 E jct US128 on MA133 (Essex Ave), (Exit 14) then 4.6 right to 138 Magnolia Ave
Franklin County								
21-06-01	Conway (RB1999)	South River	Burkeville (closed)	1	106	1870	Howe	7.6 NW jct I91 on MA116 (Exit 24), then just left on Poland Rd.
-02 #2	Greenfield	Green River	Pumping Station	1	94	1972	Howe	0.7 E jct I91 on MA2A (Exit 26), then 1.4 left on Conway St., 0.8 left (past municipal park), 0.1 right, 2.7 right on Plain Rd. and 0.3 right on Eunice Williams Dr.
-03	Colrain	North River	Arthur Smith (closed)	1	98	1870	Burr	1.2 SW of Colrain town green on MA112, then 0.1 right on Lyonville Rd.
-04 #2	Charlemont	Mill Brook	Bissell (closed) (bypassed)	1	92	1951	Long variation	0.5 N jct MA2 on MA8A.
-11	Ashfield	Creamery Brook	Creamery Brook (private)	1	40	1985	Queen	1.0 E jct MA112 on MA116, then 1.6 left on W side of Creamery Rd.
Hampden County								
21-07-01	Westfield	pond	Goodrich (foot)	1	40	1965	Town	2.2 SW of I90 on N Elm St (MA202/10) (Exit 3) then 0.6 right on Court St., 0.9 right (ahead) on Western Ave and 0.1 left on Kensington Ave. to Stanley Park.
Hampshire-Worcester Counties								
21-08-04 -14-01	Ware- Hardwick (RB 1986)	Ware River	Gilbertville	1	137	1886	Town	2.9 N jct MA9 on MA32, then 0.2 left on Bridge St.
Middlesex County								
21-09-01 River	Pepperell Waterous	Nashua	Chester H.	1	108	1963	Pratt variation	0.6 E jct MA111 on MA113, #2 then 0.2 left on E Groton St.
-02	Shirley	Mulpus Brook (not true truss)	Bull Run	1	75	1971	Town	Off MA2A, in village. Behind Bull Run Restaurant.

Number	Township	Stream	Name	Spans	Length	Year	Type	Directions
			Worcester County					
21-14-03	Sturbridge (M1952 &	Quinebaug River	Vermont (admission)	1	55	c1870	Town	0.5 W jct I86 on US20 (Exit to main entrance Sturbridge 1956) Village. Between tavern and farm area.
-04	Sturbridge	Quinebaug River	Service	2	70	1953	concrete	Same as for -14-03 Service road at south entrance.
-P1	Uxbridge	Boston & Maine Railroad		1	35	1892	Howe boxed pony	Dismantled, 1990, stored in park for future assembly.

MICHIGAN
Ionia County

Number	Township	Stream	Name	Spans	Length	Year	Type	Directions
22-34-01	Keene	Flat River	White	1	116	1896	Brown	0.1 W jct MI91 on MI44 to Cook's Corners, then 2.0 left on Lincoln Lake Rd to Smyrna. Go 3.7 right on White's Bridge Rd. (Take left fork.)
			Kent County					
22-41-01 #2	Ada	Thornapple River	Ada/ Bradfield (closed)	1	125	1980	Howe	4.7 E jct I96 on MI21, then 0.6 right on Thornapple River Rd and 0.1 right to town park.
-02	Vergennes	Flat River	Fallasburg	1	100	1871	Brown	3.2 N of MI21 and Lowell on Hudson Rd. to Fallasburg Park Rd, then right to sign and 0.7 right on Covered Bridge Rd. N Lowell
			Saginaw County					
22-73-02	Franken- muth	Cass River (private)	Zehnder Restaurant	3	239	1980	Town	Just N of Cass River Bridge on E side of MI83 (Main St)
			St. Joseph County					
22-75-01	Lockport	St. Joseph River	Langley	3	282	1887	Howe	3.0 N of MI86 and Centreville on Covered Bridge Rd.
			Wayne County					
22-82-01	Dearborn (M1937)	lagoon	Ackley (admission)	1	75	1832	Burr variation	1.4 W jct MI39 (Southfield Freeway) UA12 (Michigan Ave), then 0.6 left on Oakwood Blvd to Greenfield Village.

MINNESOTA
Goodhue County

Number	Township	Stream	Name	Spans	Length	Year	Type	Directions
23-25-01	Zumbrota	Zumbro River	Zumbrota	1	120	1869	Town variation	1.2 N jct US52 on MN58, then 0.2 left at sign For municipal campground. In Covered Bridge Park.

MISSOURI
Cape Girardeau County

Number	Township	Stream	Name	Spans	Length	Year	Type	Directions
25-16-01	Burfordville	Whitewater River	Bollinger Mill (closed)	1	140	1868	Howe	5.1 WSW jct MO72 on MO34 to Burfordville, then 0.1 left on CR "OO" and 0.3 left on CR "HH" WSW Jackson
			Jefferson County					
25-50-01	Hillsboro	Sandy Creek	Sandy Creek/ LeMay Ferry Road (closed)	1	76	1886	Howe	4.3 NNW of main intersection in Hillsboro on MO21, then 0.4 right on L LeMay Ferry Rd.

Number	Township	Stream	Name	Spans	Length	Year	Type	Directions
Laclede County								
25-53-01	Lebanon	Dry Glaze Creek	E.D. Rush (private)	1	50	1980	Howe	1.4 W I44 on Business I44 (Exit 130), then 0.3 right on Jefferson Ave, 0.2 right on Commercial St and 0.4 right (ahead) on Mill Creek Rd to end.
Linn County								
25-58-01	Laclede	Dry Channel, Locust Creek	Locust Creek (closed)	1	151	1868	Howe	1.0 N jct US36 on MO139, then 1.8 right on CR "Y" and 1.3 ahead on dead end road. ENE Meadville
Monroe County								
25-69-02	Paris	Elk Fork	Union (closed)	1	125	1871	Burr	5.4 W jct MO15 on US24, then 3.5 left on CR "C" and 0.3 right on bypassed section of unnamed road.
Gallatin County								
26-16-01	Bozeman	Hyalite Farmers Canal	Mike's	1	39	1980	Town	From Main St. in Bozeman, 7.0 S on South 19th Ave., 0.8 right on unmarked road. Take 3rd left, then left fork.

NEW HAMPSHIRE
Belknap County

Number	Township	Stream	Name	Spans	Length	Year	Type	Directions
29-01-02	Gilford	Gunstock Brook (foot)	Tannery Hill	1	42	1995	Town	2.6 S jct NH11 on NH11A then 0.1 right on Belknap Mountain Rd, and 0.2 left on Potter Hill Rd.
Carroll County								
29-02-01	Jackson	Ellis River	Jackson/ Honeymoon	1	121	1876	Paddleford and arch	2.3 N jct US302 on NH16, then 0.1 right on NH16A.
-02	Bartlett	Saco River	Bartlett (closed) (private)	1	166	1851	Paddleford and arch	1.8 W jct NH16 on N side of bypassed section of US302. West Side Rd, then just right On old Rte 16.
-05	Conway	Swift	Swift River	1	129	1870	Paddle-	0.4 N jct NH16/153 on ford E side of by passed section and arch of West Side Rd.
-06	Conway	Swift River	Albany	1	120	1858	Paddleford	4.0 WNW jct NH16 on NH12 (Kancamangus Highway), then just right at Covered Bridge Campground.
-07	Sandwich (RB1966)	Cold River	Durgin	1	96	1869	Paddleford and arch	0.9 N jct NH113 on NH13A, then 1.3 right on Fellows Hill on Fellows Hill Rd. and just left on Durgin Rd.
-08	Ossipee	Bearcamp River	Whittier/ Bearcamp (closed)	1	133	c1870	Paddleford and arch	0.6 W jct NH16 on NH25, then 0.2 right on unnamed road.
-13	Jackson	Ellis		1	115	1991	Warren	next to -02-01
Cheshire County								
29-03-02	Winchester (RB 1999)	Ashuelot River	Upper Village	2	169	1864	Town	1.7 W jct NH10 and Winchester on NH119, then 0.2 left on Old Ashuelot Rd. At Ashuelot
29-03-03	Winchester (RB 1998)	Ashuelot River	Coombs	1	107	1837	Town	4.7 N jct NH119 (east) on NH10, then 0.4 left on Coombs Bridge Rd.

Number	Township	Stream	Name	Spans	Length	Year	Type	Directions
			(cont'd) Cheshire County					
-04	Swanzey (RB 1998)	Ashuelot River Swanzey	Thompson/ West	2	137	1832	Town	3.9 S jct NH101 and Keene on NH10, then 0.3 left on Main St.
-05	Swanzey	Ashuelot River	Cresson/ Sawyer's	2	158	1859	Town	3.1 S jct NH101 and Keene on NH10, then 2.0 left on Sawyer's Crossing S. Keene
-06 #2	West Swanzey	Ashuelot River	Slate	1	145	2001	Town	5.6 S jct NH101 and Keene on NH10, then 0.4 right on old Rte 110.
-07	Swanzey (RB 1998)	South Branch, Ashuelot River	Carlton (closed)	1	67	1869	Queen	4.5 S jct NH12 and SE edge of Keene on NH32, then 0.3 left on Carleton Rd. W East Swanzey
			Coos County					
29-04-01	Pittsburg	Perry Stream	Happy Corner (closed)	1	61		Paddle-ford and arch	5.5 NE jct NH145 and Pittsburg on US3, then 0.2 right on bypassed section of Hill Rd.
-02	Pittsburg	Perry	River Road	1	51	1858	Queen	6.2 NE jct NH145 and Pittsburg on US3, then 1.2 right on River Rd.
-03	Clarksville-Pittsburg	Connecticut River	Clarksville/ Pittsburg (closed)	1	89	1876	Paddle-ford and arch	0.9 W jct NH145 and Pittsburg on US3, then 0.2 left on Bacon Rd (dead end). W Pittsburg
-04	Northumberland	Upper Ammonoosuc River	Groveton (closed)	1	126	1852	Paddle-ford and arch	Just E jct US3/NH110 on bypassed section of US3. at Groveton
-05	Stark	Upper Ammonoosuc River	Stark	1+	134	1862	Paddle-ford	6.8 E jct US3 and Groveton on NH110, then just left on village road.
-06	Lancaster	Israel River	Mechanic Street	1	94	1862	Paddle-ford	0.2 SE jct US3 (north) on US2, then 0.3 left on Mechanic Street.
-P1	Gorham	Moose Brook		1			boxed pony	1.2 W jct NH16 on US2. Park on N side of US2, walk 0.3 E on old Boston & Maine Railroad grade (bicycle trail).
-P2	Randolph	Snyder Brook		1			boxed pony	5.2 W jct NH16 on US2 to National Forest Parking Area. Walk 0.2 on old Boston & Maine Railroad grade.
			Coos County - Essex County VT					
29-04-07 45-05-02	Columbia, NH, Lemington, VT	Connecticut River	Columbia	1	146	1912	Howe	4.2 SW jct NH26 and Colebrook on US3, then 0.1 right on road to VT.
-08 -03	Lancaster, NH, Lunenburg, VT	Connecticut	Mount Orne River	2	266	1911	Howe	4.9 W jct US3 and Lancaster on NH135, then 0.1 right (ahead) on road to VT.
			Grafton County					
29-05-02	Bath (RB1989)	Wild Ammonoo- River	Swiftwater	2	158	1849	Paddle-ford and arch	2.1 SE jct US302/NH10 on NH112, then 0.1 left on suc Valley Rd. At Swiftwater

Number	Township	Stream	Name	Spans	Length	Year	Type	Directions
			(cont'd) Grafton County					
-03	Bath (RB 1988)	Ammonoosuc River/ Boston & Maine Railroad	Bath	4	375	1832	multiple King and arch	1.3 NNE jct NH112, on US302/NH10, then 1.0 left on Old Woodsville Rd.
-04	Bath-Haverhill	Ammonoosuc River	Bath-Haverhill/ Woodsville	2	256	1829	Town and arch	0.2 N jct US302 on NH135. N edge Woodsville
-05	Lincoln	Pemigewasset River	Flume (admission)	1	50	1871	Paddleford	2.5 N jct I93 (Exit 33) to entrance on E side of US3. In Flume Reservation at Franconia State Park
-07 #2	Campton	West Branch Brook	Turkey Jim	1	61	1965	Queen	1.0 W jct I93 on NH49 (Exit 28), then 0.5 right on US3 and 0.2 right At Bridge Brook Campground. (Ask at office.)
-08 #2	Campton	Beebe River	Bump	1	68	1972	Queen	At jct NH49/NH175, go 2.8 S on NH175, 0.4 left on Perch Pond Rd., 0.8 right on Branch Rd. and just left.
-09	Campton	Pemigewasset River	Blair	2	293	1869	Long and arch	0.3 E of I93 (Exit 27) on Blair Rd. NNE Plymouth
-10 #2	Plymouth	Baker River	Smith	1	149	2001	Long and arch	2.3 W jct US3 on NH25, (exit 26 of I93), then 0.6 right on Smith Bridge Rd.
-11	Lyme	Clay Brook	Edgell	1	132	1885	Town	1.6 S jct NH25A on NH10, then 0.8 right on River Rd. SSW Orford
-14 formerly (45-12-16)	Lincoln (M1964)	Pemigewasset River (admission)	Clark/ Pinsley Railroad	1	116	1904	Howe	1.0 N jct NH112 to entrance to Clark's Trading Post, on E side of US3.
-15	Grafton	Mill Brook	Brundage (private) (permission)	1	30	1957	Town	0.3 N of US4 to main intersection in E. Grafton, then 1.2 NNW to River Rd and 2.0 right to hidden driveway on W side of road.
-18	Woodstock	pond (foot)	Jack O'Lantern Resort	1	76	1987	Town	0.3 S jct I93 (Exit 30) on E side of US3 at Keating Country Club
-50 #2	Lebanon	Mascoma River	Packard Hill	1	76	2000	Howe	E I89 at Exit 17, then 0.1 left and 0.8 right on Riverside Dr.
-113	Ashland	outlet Squam Lake	Squam River	1	61	1990	Town	2.0 left left in the village Sq on US3 then 1.0 right.
			Hillsborough County					
29-06-02	Greenfield-Hancock	Contoocook River	County	1	87	1937	Pratt	2.1 SSW jct NH137 on US202, then 1.2 left on Forest Rd.
-P1	Wilton	Blood Brook		1	52		Town boxed pony	0.8 W jct NH31 (south) on NH101, then just left on Russell Hill Rd.

Number	Township	Stream	Name	Spans	Length	Year	Type	Directions
Merrimack County								
29-07-01	Andover	Blackwater River	Cilleyville (closed)	1	53	1887	Town	0.8 W jct US4, N, on NH11. On S side of highway.
-02	Andover	Blackwater River	Keniston	1	65	1882	Town	1.6 W jct US4 (south) on US4/NH11, then 0.2 left on dead end road, S from highway.
-03	Bradford	West Branch, Warner River	Bement	1	61	1854	Long	0.3 W jct NH114 on NH103, then 0.1 left on Center Rd.
-04	Warner	Warner River	Waterloo	1	76	1857	Town	1.0 W jct I89 on NH103 (Exit 9), then 0.3 left on New Market Rd.
-05	Warner	Warner River	Dalton	1	77	1853	Long and Queen	1.0 W jct I89 on NH103 then 0.2 left on Joppa Rd
-07	Hopkinton	Contoocook River	Contoocook Railroad (closed)	2	157	1889	Double Town	Just N jct NH127 on W side of NH103. On abandoned railroad right-of-way. At Contoocook
-08	Hopkinton (RB 1995)	Contoocook River	Rowell	1	140	1853	Long and arch	2.5 W of I89 (Exit 6) on Clement Hill Rd)
-09	Franklin	Winnipe-saukee River	Sulphite Railroad (arsoned, (unhoused) (on deck)	3	180	1896	Pratt	0.4 E jct NH127 on US3/NH11. Park on W side of river and walk 0.5 under railroad trestle on a gated road.
-12	Henniker	Contoocook River	New England	1	137	1972	Town	0.6 S jct US202/NH9 on NH114, then 0.1 right and 0.2 left on New England College campus.
Strafford County								
29-09-08	Dover	Cocheco River	Cocheco River (foot)	1	156	1996	Warren	Washington St., near NH9.
-P1	Dover	Boston & Maine Railroad	Rollins Farm	1	43	1904	Howe boxed pony	0.2 N jct NH4 on NH9/16, then 1.9 right on Broadway/Green Sts, 0.4 right on Rollins Rd and walk 0.3 E. opposite Clement Rd.
Sullivan County								
29-10-01	Cornish	Mill Brook	Blacksmith Shop (closed)	1	91	1881	multiple King	2.1 E of NH12A on Cornish City Rd, then 0.1 right on abandoned road.
-02	Cornish	Mill Brook	Dingleton	1	78	1882	multiple King	0.9 E of NH12A on Cornish Cornish City Rd, then 0.1 right on Root Hill Rd.
-03	Newport	Sugar River	Pier Railroad	2	217	1907	double Town-Pratt	3.7 W jct NH10 and Newport on NH11/103, then 1.2 left on N side of Chandler Mill Rd. On abandoned railroad right-of-way. (Part of bicycle trail) W Kelleyville
-04	Newport	Sugar River	Wright Railroad	1	124	1906	double Town	3.7 W jct NH10 and Newport on NH11/103, then 2.0 left on Chandler Rd to right-of-way access on N side of road. Walk 0.4 W. On abandoned railroad right-of-way. (Part of bicycle trail). W Kelleyville

Number	Township	Stream	Name	Spans	Length	Year	Type	Directions
\multicolumn{9}{c}{*(cont'd) Sullivan County*}
-05 #2	Newport	Croydon Branch, Sugar River	Corbin	1	96	1994	Town	1.7 N of NH11/103 and Newport on NH10, then 0.9 left on unnamed road.
-06	Langdon	Cold River	McDermott (closed)	1	81	1869	Town	1.3 N jct NH112A/123 on NH123A, then 0.1 left on bypassed section of road N from NH123A, on E side of road
-07	Langdon	Great Brook	Drewsville/ Prentiss (closed)	1	35	1874	Town	2.1 SE jct NH12 and South Charleston on NH12A then 0.6 right on road past Fall Mountain High School and 0.2 right on E side of bypassed section of unnamed road (parallel to NH12A).
-08	Plainfield	Blood's Brook	Meriden/ Mill	1+	80	1880	multiple King	0.9 NW of NH120 and main intersection in Meriden on Brook Rd, then 0.1 left on Colby Hill Rd. NW Meriden
-10	Cornish	Blow-Me-Down Brook	Bayliss/ Over Gorge	1	86	1877	multiple King	1.4 SW of Plainfield, US10 on NH12A, then 0.4 left on B Lang Rd. SW Plainfield
\multicolumn{9}{c}{*Sullivan County - Windsor County, VT*}
29-10-09 45-14-16	Cornish-Windsor, VT (RB 1989)	Connecticut River	Cornish-Windsor	2	449	1866	Town	0.5 N of Cornish City Rd on NH12A, then just left on Bridge St.

NEW JERSEY
Hunterdon County

Number	Township	Stream	Name	Spans	Length	Year	Type	Directions
30-10-01	Delaware	Wickeheoke Creek	Green Sergeants	1	84	1866	Queen	4.0 NE of NJ29 and Stockton on CR523 to Sergeantsville, then 1.2 left on road to Rosemont, (CR604). W Sergeantsville

NEW YORK
Albany County

Number	Township	Stream	Name	Spans	Length	Year	Type	Directions
32-01-01	New Scotland	Vly Creek	Waldbillig (private)	1	30	1955	Warren	0.7 N jct NY85A (State Farm Rd), then 1.2 right on Normanskill Rd (CR20) and 0.3 right (just before crossing creek). NE Voorheesvile
\multicolumn{9}{c}{*Brome County*}
32-04-02			Munson	1	22	1991	Queen	
\multicolumn{9}{c}{*Delaware County*}
32-13-01	Colchester	East Branch, Delaware River	Downsville	1	174	1854	Long and Queen	0.4 SSE jct NY206 (N) on NY30, then 0.1 right on Bridge St (ahead) S edge Downsville
-02	Delhi	West Branch, Delaware River	Fitches	1	100	1870	Town	3.5 NE jct NY28 and Delhi on NY10, then just right on Fitches Bridge Rd.
-03	Hamden	West Branch, Delaware River	Hamden	1+	125	1859	Long	1.5 S jct CR2 on NY10, then just left on Basin Clove Rd.

Number	Township	Stream	Name	Spans	Length	Year	Type	Directions
\multicolumn{9}{c}{*(cont'd) Delaware County*}									
-05	Middletown (M1935)	Mill Brook	Tuscarora Club/Demis (permission at lodge) (private)	1	38	1870	formerly King, now stringer	2.2 SW jct NY30 and Margaretville on NY28, then 0.3 left and 0.3 right on NYC road along Pepacton Reservoir, 2.8 left on Mill Brook Rd to D.L. Reese mailbox, and walk 0.1 right on road at telephone pole #32/125. 2.0 ahead on left.
-07	Hancock	Trout Brook	Lower Shavertown (permission) (private)	1	32	1877	Town	3.4 SE of NY17 and Roscoe on CR92 (Exit94), then 2.2 right on CR96 to N end of Tennanah Lake and 2.7 right (sharp) on Methol Rd. Bridge is on E side of road to Lake Muskoday. WSW Cooks Falls
-08	Middletown	brook	Erpf (permission) (private	1	31	1964	Town	0.2 W of CR38 and Arkville on NY28, then 0.9 left on Dry Brook Rd, 0.4 left (opposite white house) on dead end Erpf Rd, cross bridge to large house and walk 0.1 right SE Arkville
\multicolumn{9}{c}{*Essex County*}									
32-16-01	Jay (dismantled, 1997)	East Branch, Ausable River	Jay	1+	160	1857	Howe	Disassembled bridge in Jay Playground
\multicolumn{9}{c}{*Fulton County*}									
32-18-01	E. Broadalbin	Kenyatto Creek	Eagle Mills (permission)	1	41	1967	Town	5.0 E jct NY 30 and Vail on NY29, then 1.4 left on Eagle Mills Rd (CR138) and 0.2 left on road at Eagle Mills Cider Co. (open only in fall)
-03			Kwiatowski	1	44		Town and Queen	
\multicolumn{9}{c}{*Herkimer County*}									
32-22-01	Salisbury	Spruce Creek	Salisbury Center	1	50	1875	multiple King and arch	0.1 SE jct NY29A on NY29, then 0.1 right on Fairview Rd.
\multicolumn{9}{c}{*Jefferson County*}									
32-23-01	Belleville	pond	Frontenac/ North Country (private) (ask permission) from Gary Beckstead, Rte 1, Box 577, Adams, NY 13605)	1	44	1982	Town	4.5 N of NY289 and Bellevile on E side of CR75.
\multicolumn{9}{c}{*Madison County*}									
32-27-01	Madison	Mill Pond	Americana Village (private)	1	33	1968	Warren	3.0 SSW of US20 and Madison on E side of Lake Moraine Rd. (CR83).
\multicolumn{9}{c}{*Otsego County*}									
32-39-01	Springfield	Shadow Brook	Hyde Hall	1	53	1825	Burr	4.5 S of US20 and East Springfield to entrance on W side of CR31 on East Lake Rd in Glimmerglass State Park.
\multicolumn{9}{c}{*Rensselaer-Washington Counties*}									
32-42-02 -58-04	Hoosick- White Creek	Hoosick River	Buskirk	1	164	1880	Howe	3.5 W jct NY22 (north) on NY67 then 0.3 right on C103/59. At Buskirk

Number	Township	Stream	Name	Spans	Length	Year	Type	Directions
			Saratoga County					
32-46-01	Edinburg	Beecher Creek	Copeland (closed) (private)	1	35	1879	Queen	0.6 W of west end of Batchelerville Bridge (Scanandaga Lake) on CR98, then 0.3 right on Military Rd (CR4) to Edinburg and 0.2 right on North Shore Rd (CR4).
			Scoharie County					
32-48-01	Blenheim	Scoharie Creek	Blenheim (double-barrel)	1	210	1855	Long and arch	0.3 E of CR31 and North Blenheim on NY30, then 0.1 right on bypassed section of NY30.
			Suffolk County					
32-52-01	Southampton	man made pond	Ludlow Green's	1	51	1990	Town	Left on Norris Lane from NY27, 0.1 right on Sawassett Ave. Bridgehampton
			Sullivan County					
32-53-01	Neversink	Neversink River	Halls Mills (closed) (abandoned)	1	119	1912	Town	2.7 N of NY55 and Curry on C19, then 0.3 left to bypassed section of Hunter Rd. Walk 0.2 S. N Curry
-02	Rockland	Beaverkill Creek	Beaverkill/ Conklin	1	98	1865	Town	0.3 W of NY17 on CR82 (Exit 96), then 1.3 right on old Rte 17 (CR179), 4.8 right on Beaverkill Rd (CR151). 0.5 left on Beaverkill Camp Rd and 0.1 right on Campsite Rd to Beaverkill State Campsite. SW Lewis Beach
-03	Rockland	Willowemoc Creek	Van Tran Flat/ Livingston Manor	1	117	1860	Town and arch	0.3 W of NY17 on CR82 (Exit 96), then 1.0 right on old Rte 17 (CR179) and 0.3 left on Covered Bridge Rd. N Livingston Manor
-04	Rockland	Willowemoc Creek	Bendo	1	48	1860	Town	5.6 E of NY17 on CR82 (Exit 96) to Debruce, then 1.8 right on Willowemoc Rd and 0.4 right on Conklin Hill Rd to Covered Bridge Campsites. WSW Willowemoc
			Tompkins County					
32-55-01	Newfield (RB1972)	West Branch, Cayuga Creek	Newfield	1	115	1853	Town and arch	2.6 SW jct NY34/96 on NY NY13, then 0.8 right at Newfield exit old Rte. 13) and 0.1 right onBridge St. (between Main and Bank Sts).
			Ulster County					
32-56-01	Esopus-Rosendale	Wallkill River	Perrine (closed)	1	154	1844	Burr	0.3 E jct NY32 on N side of bypassed section of NY213. (adjacent to I87 but no access) SW Rifton
-02	Hardenbergh	Dry Brook	Forge (private) (permission)	1	27	1906	King	0.2 W of CR38 and Arkville on NY28, then 7.6 left on Dry Brook Rd and just right. N Seager

Number	Township	Stream	Name	Spans	Length	Year	Type	Directions
			Ulster County					
-03	Hardenbergh (RB1985)	Dry Brook	Tappan/ Kittle (without functional truss)	1	43	1906	King	0.2 W of CR38 and Arkville on NY28, then 8.5 left on Dry Brook Rd and just left on Erickson Rd. N Seager
-05	Olive (M1930)	Old Channel, Esopus Creek	Ashokan/ Turnwood (private)	1	62	1889	Town	1.5 NE of NY213 and Olivebridge on NY28A, then 1.0 right on Beaverkill Rd to main gate of New Paltz Campus of NY State Univ, then 0.1 right to parking area and walk 0.5 S. E Olivebridge
-06	Hardenbergh	Mill Brook	Grants' Mills	1	66	1902	Town	2.2 SW jct NY30 and Margaretville on NY28, then 0.3 left and 0.3 right on NYC road along Pepacton Reservoir and 5.0 left on N side of bypassed section of Mill Brook Rd. S Margaretville
			Washington County					
32-58-01	Jackson-Salem	Batten Kill	Eagleville	1	101	1858	Town	3.4 SE of VT State line on NY313, then 0.3 right on Eagleville Rd. Eagleville
-02	Jackson-Salem	Batten Kill	Shushan (closed) (private museum)	2	161	1858	Town	4.0 S jct NY29 on NY22, then 2.0 left on N side of bypassed section of CR61. Shushan
-03	Jackson-Salem (RB1984)	Batten Kill	Rexleigh	1	107	1874	Howe	0.3 ENE jct NY29 on NY22 to Greenwich Jct, then 1.5 right on Rexleigh Rd. SSW Salem

NORTH CAROLINA
Bertie County

Number	Township	Stream	Name	Spans	Length	Year	Type	Directions
33-08-01	Windsor	Coniott Creek	Rasco Mills (private) (mill bridge structure)	1	16	c1860	stringer	0.8 S jct NC308 on US13BP, 5.5 right on CR1100 (to Grubtown), 3.1 right on CR1108 (to Quintana) and 1.6 right ahead), then 1.8 left on CR121 (dead end road).
-02	Windsor	Hoggard Mill Creek	Hoggard Grist Mill (private)	2	27		stringer	0.4 N jct US13BP (north) on US13, 0.6 right on CR1301 to CR1300, then just ahead on E side of CR1301.
-03	Windsor	Hoggard Mill Creek	Hoggard Saw Mill	1	39		stringer	Same as for -08-02)

Catawba County

Number	Township	Stream	Name	Spans	Length	Year	Type	Directions
33-18-01	Claremont	Lyle Creek	Bunker Hill (closed)	1	85	1894	Haupt	2.2 W jct NC10 on abandoned section of old Rte 64/70. Park on N side of of road and walk 0. 0.3 N on footpath.

Forsyth County

Number	Township	Stream	Name	Spans	Length	Year	Type	Directions
33-34-01	Old Salem	dry land	Museum (foot)	1	120	1998	modified Burr	At Museum of Early Southern Decorative Arts, off NC52.

Number	Township	Stream	Name	Spans	Length	Year	Type	Directions
			Randolph County					
33-76-01	Pisgah	Upper Branch, Little River	Pisgah (closed)	3	51	c1910	stringer	1.0 N jct US220 BP (south) on Business US220 to Ulah, 7.0 left on CR1114 to Pisgah and 2.0 right on bypassed section of CR1109 in roadside park.
			OHIO *Adams County*					
35-01-02	Oliver	Cherry Fork, Ohio Brush Creek	Harshaville	1+	110	c1855	King and arch	multiple 1.5 S jct OH32 (Appalachian Highway) on OH247, then 1.0 left on Grace's Run Rd (CR1). SE Seamen
-10	Liberty	East Fork, Eagle Creek	Kirker (closed) (bypassed)	1	63	1890	multiple King	1.6 N jct OH41 on E side of highway on bypassed section of OH136. W West Union
			Ashtabula County					
35-04-03	Plymouth	Ashtabula River (RB1993)	Olin/ Dewey Road	1+	115	1873	Town	3.7 ENE jct OH11/46 on OH84, then 1.8 right on Dewey Rd (TR334) and 0.2 left on Hadlock Rd TR335). ESE Ashtabula
-05	Conneaut (RB1995)	Conneaut Creek	Creek Road	1+	112		Town	0.1 NW jct OH84 on OH193, then 4.5 right on Creek Rd (TR443). ENE Kingsville
-06	Conneaut (RB 1984)	Conneaut Creek	Middle Road	1+	136	1868	Howe	1.1 S jct I90 on OH7 (Exit 247, then 1.2 left on South Ridge Rd (CR22) and 0.2 right on Middle Rd (TR425). SSE Conneaut
-09	Monroe	West Branch, Ashtabula River	Root Road	1+	97	1868	Town	2.0 S jct OH84 on OH7, then 2.4 right on Root Rd (TR414) WSW Monroe Center
-12	Sheffield (RB1985)	Ashtabula River	Benetka Road	1	115	c1900	Town and arch	1.6 S jct OH84 on OH193, then 1.3 right on Plymouth Ridge Rd (CR20) and 0.4 left on Benetka Rd (TR350). SSW Kingsville
-13	Pierpont (M1972)	dry land	Graham Rd (closed)	1	85	1867	Town	1.2 N jct OH167 (east) on OH7, then 1.8 left on Graham Rd (TR343). In park on S side of road.
-14	Denmark	Mill Creek	South Denmark Road (closed)	1	80	1868	Town	1.3 E jct OH11 on OH167, then 1.4 right on Mill Creek Rd (TR284) and 0.3 right on S side of bypassed section of South Denmark Rd (CR291) NW Jefferson
-16	Jefferson (RB1988)	Mill Creek	Mullen/ Doyle Road	1	84	1876	Town and arch	1.1 W jct OH46 on OH307, then 0.8 right on Doyle Rd (TR287).
-18	Austinburg	Grand River	Mechanicsville (bypassed)	1	154	1867	Howe and arch	2.4 W jct OH45 on OH307, then 0.8 left on E side of bypassed section of Mechanicsville Rd (CR9). SW Austinburg

Number	Township	Stream	Name	Spans	Length	Year	Type	Directions
			Ashtabula County					
-19	Harpersfield	Grand River	Harpersfield	2+	234	1868	Howe	0.3 W jct OH534 on OH307, then 0.3 left on old Rte 534 (CR154)
-22	Morgan	Grand River	Riverdale Road	1+	120	1874	Town	0.9 N of main intersection in Rock Creek on OH45, then 0.8 left on Riverdale Rd (TR69).
-25	Windsor	Phelps Creek	Warner Hollow (closed)	3	120	1867	Town	1.6 W jct OH534 on US322, then 0.1 left on Wiswell Rd (TR357) W Orwell
-58	Monroe	Conneaut Creek	State Road	2	157	1983	Town	2.3 W jct OH7 on OH84, then 1.6 right on State Rd (CR354) N Kelloggsville
-61	Pierpont	West Branch, Ashtabula River	Caine Road	1	96	1986	Pratt	2.4 W jct OH7 (north) and OH167 (east) on Caine Rd (TR579). WNW Pierpont
-62	Jefferson	Mill Creek	Giddings Road	1	107	1995	Pratt	1.0 W jct OH11 on OH167, 0.9 N on TR295, then 0.5 left on Jones Rd (TR294) and 0.4 on Giddings Rd. NE Jefferson
-63	Jefferson	Mill Creek	Netcher Road	1	108	1999	inverted Haupt	2.0 W jct OH193 on Netcher Rd. E Jefferson
			Athens County					
35-05-01	Trimble	Sunday Creek	Palos	1+	75	1875	multiple King	1.3 N jct OH78 on OH13, then 0.1 right on Trimble Rd (TR347, Sec 4). NNW Glouster
-02	Dover	Sunday Creek	Kidwell (closed)	1	96	1880	Howe	0.7 S jct OH685 on OH13, 0.2 right on dead end TR332 (Sec 4). SSW Jacksonville
-06	Lodi	Middle Branch, Shade River	Blackwood	1+	64	1881	multiple King	Just N of Meigs County line on US33, then 1.8 right (ahead) on King Rd (CR45), 3.7 right on Bucks Lake Rd (CR44) and 0.7 right on Blackwood Rd (CR46, Sec 1). ENE Pratts Fork
			Auglaize County					
35-06-54	St. Marys	St. Marys River	Memorial Park (foot)	1	105	1992	Howe	In St. Marys, near center of town. Off OH66, on N side of South St. In Memorial Park.
			Belmont County					
35-07-05 formerly -23-46	Richland (M1973)	lake	Shaeffer/ Campbell (closed)	1	68	1875	multiple King	0.2 N jct I70 on OH331 (Exit 213), then 0.1 left on unmarked road, Twp-Sec 2 8 On Ohio Univ. Belmont campus. W St. Clairsville
			Brown County					
35-08-04	Pike/Scott	White Oak Creek	Brown (closed) (bypassed)	1	129	1878	Smith	2.5 NE of US68 and main intersection in New Hope on New Hope-White Oak Station Rd (CR5).
-05	Scott	White Oak Creek (closed) (bypassed)	New Hope/ Bethel Road	1	172	1878	Howe and arch	0.2 S of main intersection in New Hope on US68, then 0.1 right on N side of bypassed section of Bethel-New Hope Rd. (CR5)

Number	Township	Stream	Name	Spans	Length	Year	Type	Directions
			(cont'd) Brown County					
-08	Perry	East Fork, Little Miami	McCafferty River	1	157	1877	Howe	2.3 SW jct OH131 on US50, then 0.1 left on McCafferty Rd (CR105). SW Fayetteville
-23	Huntington-Union	Eagle Creek	North Pole Road (closed)	1	156	1875	Smith	Off US62/68, 1.4 NE jct US52, then 3.0 right and 0.2 left on North Pole Rd (CR13). ENE Ripley
-34	Byrd	West Fork, Eagle Creek	George Miller	1	154	1879	Smith	1.2 S jct OH125 on US62, then 1.8 left and 0.6 left (ahead) on George Miller Rd (CR15). SE Russellville
			Butler County					
35-09-02	Morgan (M1966)	Ravine	State Line/ Bebb Park (closed) (bypassed)	1	120	1868	Wernwag	0.9 SE jct OH129 on OH126, then 0.7 right on TR-Sec 6 in Bebb Park. SSE Scipio
-03	Oxford	Four Mile Creek	Black/ Pugh's Mill (closed) (bypassed)	1+	206	1868	Childs	0.8 N jct US27 on OH732, then 0.3 left on Corso Rd to dead end on bypassed section of OH732.
			Carroll County					
35-10-14	Center	Indian (private)	Indian Fork	1	30	1996	multiple King	1.0 SSE of Carrollton at 190 Alamo Rd. on Blue Bird Farm. Walk back on nature trail.
			Clermont County					
35-13-02	Stonelick	Stonelick Creek	Perintown/ Stonelick	1	140	1878	Howe	0.2 W jct OH222 on US50, then 1.0 right and 0.3 left on Stonelick Creek Rd (CR116) E Perintown
			Clinton County					
35-14-09	Clark	Todd's Fork, Miami River	Martinsville Road	1	72	1871	multiple King	1.8 W jct OH134 on OH28, then 0.6 right on Martinsville Rd. (CR14). WNW Martinsville
			Clinton-Highland Counties					
35-14-11 / -36-06	Clark/	East Fork, Dodson River	Lynchburg Miami (closed)	1	120	1870	Long	0.5 N jct OH135 on OH134, then 0.2 left on High St and just ahead on Covered Bridge Ln. W edge Lynchburg
			Columbiana County					
35-15-01 #2	Center Sect. 33 (RB1994)	dry land	Sells/Roller Mill	1	50	1994	multiple King	1.0 W of center of town on US30, then left on TR764 (Wayne Bridge Rd), 2.8 right to Scenic Vista Park SW of Lisbon
-02	Center	West Fork, Little Beaver Creek	McClellan (abandoned) (closed)	1	53	1871	multiple King	1.6 W jct OH164 on OH518, then 1.4 right on Trinity Church Rd. (TR756) and walk 0.1 right on McClellan Rd (TR871-Sec 32)
-05	Salem	Middle Fork, Little Beaver Creek	Teegarden/ Centennial (closed) (bypassed)	1	66	1876	multiple King	2.4 NW jct US30 on OH45, then 2.7 left on E side of bypassed section of Eagleton Rd (TR761-Sec 32). NW Lisbon

Number	Township	Stream	Name	Spans	Length	Year	Type	Directions
			(Cont'd) Columbiana County					
-08	Elk Run (M1982)	dry land	Church Hill Road (closed)	1	19	1870	King	1.4 E jct US30/OH11 on S side of OH154, (TR Sec 2) adjacent to Lock 24 Restaurant. W edge Elkton
-96	Middleton (M1971)	Gaston Mill Tailrace	Thomas J. Malone (closed)	1	42	1870	multiple King (altered truss)	2.1 N jct US30/OH11 on OH 7, then 1.2 right Bell School Rd. (TR1131) and 1.4 left In Beaver Creek State Park. N East Liverpool
			Coshocton County					
35-16-02	Clark #2	Killbuck	Helmick Creek	2	166	1996	multiple King	1.3 ESE OH60 and Blissfield on CR25, then just left on TR25 - Sec 18. ESE Blissfield
			Cuyahoga County					
35-18-01	Olmstead	Plum Creek	Charles A. Harding Memorial	1	92	1998		On Main St., one block E of OH252
			Delaware County					
35-21-04	Porter	Big Walnut Creek	Chambers Road	1+	73	1883	Childs	0.4 NE jct OH521 on OH656. then 1.0 left on Lott Rd. (TR64) and 0.2 right on Chambers Rd (TR63). NNE Olive Green
			Fairfield County					
35-23-07	Violet Sect. 25 (M1986)	Sycamore Creek	Hizey/ Visintine (private)	1	83	1891	multiple King and Queen	4.3 E jct OH256 on OH204, then 1.0 right and 0.1 right at 12549 Tollgate Rd, NW. NE Pickerington
-10	Pleasant Sect. 30 (M1988)	Fetter's Run	Jon Bright #2 (closed)	1	75	1881	inverted bowstring and arch	2.0 N jct US22 on E side of OH37 on Ohio University, Lancaster campus. N Lancaster
-15	Madison	Clear Sect. 9	Hannaway Creek (closed) (by passed)	1	86	1901	multiple King	From E edge of Amanda, go 0.3 on OH159, then 3.4 left on Amanda-Clearport Rd (CR69) and 0.4 right on E side of bypassed section of Clearport Rd (CR24). S Clearport
-16	Madison	Clear Sect 10	Johnson Creek (closed) (bypassed)	1	98	1887	Howe	From E edge of Amanda go 0.3 S on OH159, then 5.0 left on Amanda-Clearport Rd (CR69). ESE Clearport
-19	Violet Sect. 10 (M1986)	Sycamore Creek	Zeller-Smith (closed)	1	79	1906	multiple King and Queen	Follow OH256 into Pickerington, go1 block N of stop light, 0.2 right on Lockville (Pickerington) Rd, to access park at S end of concrete bridge. Go left into Sycamore Creek Park. SE edge Pickerington
-20	Berne (M1979)	dry land	Shade (closed) (permission) (private) (rebuilt without truss members)	1	122	1871		0.4 E US33 to Sugar Grove, then 0.3 right (across bridge). 1.6 right on Buckeye Rd. (TR400) and 0.5 left on S side of Sullivan Rd (TR298) Bill Pierson Farm. SE Sugar Grove

Number	Township	Stream	Name	Spans	Length	Year	Type	Directions
			(cont'd) Fairfield County					
-25	Greenfield (M1987)	dry land	McLeery (closed) (permission) (private) (shortened from original length)	1	52	1864	multiple King	2.4 S jct OH256 on OH158, then 0.2 right on S side of Pleasantville Rd (CR17) (on James Walters Property) S Baltimore
-27	Liberty (M1987)	ditch	Shryer (closed) (permission) (private)	1	65	1891	multiple King variation (skewed)	1.0 W of OH158 on OH256, then 3.3 left on N side of Basil-Western Rd (CR13). (on Bill Shryer Farm) W Baltimore
-30	Walnut (M1982)	dry land	Charles Holliday (closed)	1	98	1897	multiple King variation	0.2 S of OH204 (west) on Lancaster St (past US Post Office) then 0.5 left on Chatauqua Blvd to Gate 4 of Corn Festival. Walk 0.2 S. SE edge Millersport
-33	Richland (M1981)	pond	R. F. Baker (closed)	1	66	1871	multiple King	2.2 W jct OH664 on US22, then walk 0.3 S across athletic field at at rear of Fairfield Union High School. W Rushville
-37	Pleasant (M1974)	dry land	Jon Raab (closed) (permission) (private) (guests must register)	1	44	1891	Queen	1.6 NE jct OH37 on US22, then 1.0 right to driveway on S side of TR344 at 5695 Ireland Rd. ENE Lancaster
-38	Violet (M1967)	Ohio & Erie Canal bed	Hartman #2	1	48	1888	Queen	1.5 W of US33 and traffic signal on Winchester Pike (CR23), then 1.4 right on W side of Pickerington Rd (CR20) in Lockport Village Park, NW Carroll
-43	Hocking	Arney Run	Mink Hollow (bypassed) (closed)	1	51	1887	multiple King	0.8 ESE of Clearport Rd (CR24) on Amanda-Clearport Rd (CR69), then 0.3 left and 2.2 right on Crooks Rd CR28). NE Clearport
-48	Bloom	Hocking River	Rock Mill	1	37	1901	Queen	2.7 W of US33 and Hooker traffic signal on Lithopolis Rd (CR39). then 0.1 left on Rock Mill Rd (CR41). WNW Lancaster
-49	Greenfield (M1972)	dry land	Roley School House (closed)	1	49	1899	multiple King	0.7 N jct US22 on OH37, then 0.2 left on E Fair Ave and just right at N Broad St entrance to County Fairgrounds. Lancaster
			Franklin County					
35-25-03	Madison	Walnut Creek	Bergstresser/ Dietz	1	134	1887	Partridge	0.3 N of Lithopolis Rd on OH674, then left (W) on Ashbrook Rd. S Canal Winchester
-147 (formerly -60-28)	Norwich	ravine (foot only)	Weaver Park	1	31	1993	Town	2.1 W jct I270 on Hilliard-Cemetery Rd, then 0.4 right on Norwich St., 0.2 right on Columbia St. to Weaver Park and Franklin County Fairgrounds. Bridge is on left behind a white church. W Columbus

Number	Township	Stream	Name	Spans	Length	Year	Type	Directions
Greene County								
35-29-01	Miami (M1975)	Yellow Springs Creek	Cemetery Road (closed) (shortened from original length)	1	60	1886	Howe	0.3 SW jct OH343 on US68, then 0.9 left on Corry St. and 0.6 left on W side of Grinnel Rd (CR27) on Glen Helen Nature Preserve. SSE Yellow Springs
-03	Caesar Creek	Anderson Fork, Caesar Creak	West Engle Mill Road (closed) (bypassed)	1	135	1877	Smith	0.9 NE jct OH725 on US42, then 4.2 right on Spring Valley-Painterville Rd (CR75) oand 0.5 right on bypassed section of Engle Mill Rd (TR46). ESE Spring Valley
-15	Xenia	Massie's Creek	Stevenson Road	1	98	1877	Smith	0.6 S jct OH235 on US68, 1.8 left on Brush Row Rd (TR17) and 0.5 left on Stevenson Rd (CR76).
-16	Xenia	Massie's Creek	Charleton Mill Rd	1	119	1883	Howe	2.2 WSW jct OH72 on US42, 0.9 right on Charleton Mill Rd (TR29) WSW Cedarville
-18	New Jasper	North Branch, Caesar Creek	Ballard Road	1	80	1883	Howe	4.8 WNW jct OH72 on US3 US35, then 0.5 left on Ballard Rd (TR6) WNW Jamestown
Guernsey County								
35-30-04	Knox	Indian Camp Run	Indian Camp	1	36		multiple King	5.6 NNW jct OH209 on OH658, then 0.1 right on Knox Rd (TR68-sec 12). NNW Cambridge
-12	Cambridge	ravine (M1966)	Armstrong/ Clio (closed)	1	76	1849	multiple King	1.1 N of US22/40 (Wheeling Ave) between 6th and 8th Sts. on N side of access road to Cambridge City Park.
Hamilton County								
35-31-01	Springfield Sect 28	West Fork, Mill Creek	Jediah Hill/ Groff Mill (altered height and width)	1	44	1850	Queen	1.3 N of Compton Rd (main intersection) in Mt. Healthy on US127, then 0.2 right on Miles Rd and just right on Covered Bridge Rd.(In north suburban Cincinnati.)
Harrison County								
35-34-19	Freeport Sect 16	Skull Fork, Stillwater Creek	Skull Fork (closed)	1	45		multiple King	0.8 S jct OH342 on OH800, then 1.8 right on Skull Fork Rd. (CR27) and 0.2 left on N side of Covered Bridge Rd.
Jackson County								
35-40-06	Scioto Sect 31	Brushy Fork, Little Scioto River	Crabtree/ Johnson Road	1	71	1870	Smith	7.0 SW jct OH32 (Appalachian Highway) on OH776, then 0.4 left (sharp) and 0.2 left (ahead) on Johnson Rd (TR291). SW Jackson
-08	Washington Sect 7	Pigeon Creek	Byer (closed)	1	74	1872	Smith	8.0 NW jct OH93 on OH327, then 0.1 left on CR31. NNW Wellston
-11	Milton Sect 26	Little Raccoon Creek	Buckeye Furnace	1	59	1871	Smith	4.0 E jct OH327 on OH124, then 2.0 right on Buckeye Furnace Rd (CR58) and 0.6 right at Buckeye Furnace on TR165. SSE Wellston

Number	Township	Stream	Name	Spans	Length	Year	Type	Directions
			Lawrence County					
35-44-05	Windsor Sect 13 (RB1991)	Indian Guyan Creek	Scottown/ Pleasant Ridge	1	79	1877	multiple King variation	0.8 E jct OH775 on OH217, then just right on Pleasant Ridge Rd (CR67). E Scottown
			Licking County					
35-45-04	Eden Sect 22 (M1974)	Rocky Fork, Creek	Boy Scout Camp (closed) (private)	1	49		multiple King	0.2 N of OH79 and Rocky Fork on Rainrock Rd (TR244), then 0.4 left on TR210 (Rocky Fork Rd) and 0.6 ahead to entrance on left. (Winter entrance). Walk 0.3 to bridge. NNW Rocky Fork
-05	Fallsburg Sect. 4	Wakatomika Creek	Mercer/ Girl Scout Camp	1	68	1879	multiple King	2.5 NW jct OH79 on OH586, then 1.1 right on Girl Scout Rd. (TR225). NNW Fallsburg
-06	Fallsburg Sect. 8 (RB 1993)	Wakatomika Creek	Gregg (concrete floor)	1+	124	1881	multiple King	1.4 NW jct OH79 on OH586, then 1.2 right on Frampton Rd (CR201). N Fallsburg
-17	St. Albans	dry land	Lobdell Park/ McLain (closed)	1	47	1871	multiple King	0.5 N jct OH161 on W side of OH37 in Fireman's Park. S edge Alexandria
-25	Mary Ann	Rocky Fork, Licking River	Davis Farm (private)	1	50	1947	multiple King	0.2 S of main intersection in Hickman on OH79, then 1.0 left on W side of Hickman Rd (CR210) on private road.
-160	Union	unnamed creek	Canal- Greenway (foot only)	1	70	1992	Town	2.5 SW of Hebron and US40 on Canal Rd. (TR171), then just right across from Fish Hatchery, on abandoned railroad. SW Hebron
			Logan County					
35-46-01	Bloomfield-Washington (RB 2000)	Great Miami River	McColly	1	125	1876	Howe	3.0 S jct OH274 on OH235, then 0.8 right on CR13. SW Lewistown
-03	Richland	South Fork, Great Miami River	Bickham	1	94	1877	Howe	2.6 E jct US33 on OH366, then 0.3 left on CR38. E Russell's Poin
			Miami County					
35-55-01	Concord-Staunton	Great Miami River	Eldean (bypassed)	2	225	1860	Long	1.2 SE jct I75 on OH41 then 2.3 left on old OH125 (CR25) and 0.1 right on bypassed section of Eldean Rd (CR33). N Troy
			Monroe County					
35-56-14	Perry	Little Muskingum River	Foraker	1	92	1886	multiple King	3.6 ESE of OH26 and Graysville onTrail Run Rd (CR12), then 1.0 left on Plainview Rd (CR40) ESE Graysville
-18	Washington (RB1996)	Little Muskingum River	Long/ Knowlton (closed)	3+	192	1887	multiple King and arch	2.5 S jct OH537 on OH26, then 0.3 left on TR38 to dead end at Covered Bridge Park. N Rinard Mills

Number	Township	Stream	Name	Spans	Length	Year	Type	Directions
Montgomery County								
35-57-01	German	Little Twin Creek	Germantown (closed)	1	100	1865	inverted Bowstring	0.5 W jct OH4 on OH725, then 0.1 right on N Plum St and 0.2 right on E Center St. Germantown
-03 (formerly -29-09)	Dayton (M1948)	Miami and Erie Canal bed	Feedwire Road (closed) (private)	1	42	1870	Warren and arch	0.9 E of I75 on US35 (Exit 52), then 1.5 right at Main St./Patterson Blvd exit to Carillon Historical Park. Dayton
-36 (formerly -29-26)	German	Mud Lick Creek	Jasper Road/Mud Lick (closed) (private)	1	50	1869	Warren and arch	2.5 W jct OH4 on OH725, then 0.9 left on Signal Rd and ahead 0.2 at stop sign, bridge is on left. SW edge Germantown
Morgan County								
35-58-15	Marion	Wolf Creek	Barkhurst Mill (private)	1	81	1872	multiple King and arch	1.7 N jct OH555 on OH377, then 1.0 right on CR52 and 0.4 right (ahead) on TR21, dead end road. NE Chesterhill
-32	Malta (M1953)	dry land	Rosseau (closed)	1	58		multiple King	0.5 S jct OH60 on E side of OH376 in County Fairgrounds. SE edge McConnelsville
-35	Deerfield	Island Run	Helmick Mill	1	74	1867	multiple King	2.5 W of Eagleport on OH669, then 1.7 left on TR201 and just left on TR269-sect 2. SE Eagleport
-38	Union	Branch of Sunday (closed)	Adams/San Toy	1	58	1875	multiple King	3.2 S jct OH37 on OH555, then 0.5 right on CR16 Creek and 0.1 ahead.
-41 (formerly -61-27)	Manchester Sect/ 7 (M1965)	Brannon's Fork	Milton Dye (closed) (private)	1	41	1915	multiple King	4.2 NE jct OH78 on OH83 (north), then 0.5 right on Sawmill Rd and 0.1 right on campsite loop. NE Bristol at Ohio Power Co. Campsite "D"
Muskingum County								
35-60-31	Perry	Salt Creek	Johnson Mill/Salt Creek (closed) (bypassed)	1	87	1876	Warren	2.6 E jct OH797 on US22/40, then 1.9 left on Arch Hill Rd on S side of road. ENE Zanesville
Noble County								
35-61-33	Sharon	Olive Green Creek	Manchester (closed) (bypassed)	1	49	1915	multiple King	4.5 W jct I77 on OH78 (Exit 25), then 0.9 left on CR9 and 1.5 right on TR36. S Olive Green
-34	Sharon	Sharon Fork, Olive Green Creek	Parrish (closed) (bypassed)	1+	81	1914	multiple King	2.1 W jct I77 on OH78 (Exit 25), then 2.6 left on E side of bypassed section o of CR8. SSW Sharon
-40	Olive (M1970)	ravine	Rich Valley/Park Hill	1	44		multiple King	0.1 E jct I77 on OH78 (Exit 25), then 0.3 left on Park Hill Rd County Fairgrounds. SW edge Caldwell
Perry County								
35-64-01	Hopewell Sect. 26/27	Painter Creek	Parks/South	1	58	1883	multiple King	2.6 NNE jct US22 on OH668, then 0.9 left on Gower Rd (CR33). N Somerset

Number	Township	Stream	Name	Spans	Length	Year	Type	Directions
			(cont'd) **Perry County**					
-03	Hopewell Sect. 22	Painter Creek	Hopewell Church	1	55	1874	multiple King	2.6 NNE jct US22 on OH668, then 2.0 left on Gower Rd (CR33) and 0.3 right on Cooperrider's Rd (CR51) N Somerset
-05	Madison	Kent's Run	Jack's Hollow	1	60	1879	multiple King	1.9 N of OH204 and Mt. Perry on Gratiot Rd (CR34, then 1.9 right on Kroft Rd (CR67) and 0.8 left on TR108, sect. 3. NE Mt Perry
-06	Pike (M1987)	dry land	Bowman Mill/ Redington (closed)	1+	82		multiple King	0.3 W jct OH13 on W side of OH37 at entrance to County Fairgrounds. W New Lexington
-84 (formerly 23-31)	Thorn Sect/ 26 (M1986)	pond	Ruffner/ Moore (private)	1	78	1875	Smith	7.0 S jct I70 (Exit132) or 1.0 N jct OH256 on E side of OH13 (374 Somerset Rd) SSE Thornville
			Pickaway County					
35-65-15 (formerly 23-44)	Scioto (M1978)	pond	Valentine (private) (permission)	1	36	1887	multiple King	4.0 SSE jct US62/OH3 on OH762, then 0.6 right on Thrailkill Rd (TR152) and walk 0.3 S. SSE Orient on Bill Green Farm.
-16 (formerly -60-08, -25-65)	Circleville (M1999)		Blackburn/ Brannon/ Wesner	1	60	1885	multiple King	In Buzzard Roost area of Slate Run Metro Park
			Preble County					
35-68-03	Dixon	Four Mile Creek	Harshman	1	104	1894	Childs	Take OH122, 7.3 W from Eaton, then 3.0 S on Concord-Fairhaven Rd (TR218)
-04	Harrison (M1964)	dry land	Dixon Branch (closed)	1	50	1887	Childs	0.4 N jct I79 on OH503 (Exit 14), then 0.5 right on N side of Salem Rd (CR15) to Civitan Park. E edge Lewisburg
-05	Gasper (RB1991)	Seven Mile Creek	Roberts (closed) (double)	1	79	1829	Burr	One block N of OH732 on US127 (Barron St), then one block W on St. Clair St., N on S. Beech St. On left side. Eaton
-06	Gratis	Sam's Run	Brubaker	1	85	1887	Childs	0.5 WNW jct OH725 on OH122, then 0.6 left on Brubaker Rd (TR328). WNW Gratis
-10	Washington (M1958)	dry land	Tyler/Sloane (private) (permission) (closed)	1	118	1891	Childs	4.5 NW Eaton on Eaton-Gettysburg Rd (CR11), then left at Kramer Farm.
-12	Washington	Seven Mile Creek	Christman	1	92	1895	Childs	1.0 N jct US35 on US127, then 0.5 left, 1.1 right on Eaton-Gettysburg Rd (CR11), then just left on Eaton-New Hope Rd (TR142). NW Eaton

Number	Township	Stream	Name	Spans	Length	Year	Type	Directions
			(cont'd) Preble County					
-13	Monroe	Price Creek	Geeting	1	100	1894	Childs	0.4 N jct I70 on OH503, (Exit 14), then 2.9 left on Lewisburg-Western Rd (TR436) and 0.1 ahead on Price Rd. (TR Sec 25/36). W Lewisburg
-14	Harrison	Swamp Creek	Warnke	1	52	1895	Childs	0.4 E jct OH503 on US40, then 1.6 left on Verona Rd (TR404) and 0.3 right on Swamp Creek Rd (TR403. Sec 14/23) NNE Lewisburg
			Ross County					
35-71-02	Buckskin	Buckskin Creek	Buckskin	1	99	1873	Smith	2.2 S jct OH28 on OH41, then 2.2 left on Lower Twin Rd. (CR54). W edge South Salem
			Sandusky County					
35-72-01	Ballville	East Branch, Wolf Creek	Mull (closed) (bypassed)	1+	100	1842	Town	2.2 S jct OH12 on OH53, then 1.0 right on S side of bypassed section Mull Rd (TR9 Sec 31). SSW Fremont
			Scioto County					
35-73-15	Brush Creek	Brush Creek	Otway (bypassed)	1	127	1874	Smith	0.2 W jct OH73 then 0.1 right on bypassed section of OH348. W edge Otway
			Summit County					
35-77-01 #2	Boston	Furnace Run	Everett Road (closed)	1	100	1986	Smith	0.7 E of I77 on Wheatley Rd. (TR174), then 1.2 right on Revere Rd. (TR114) and 1.6 left on Everett Rd (CR42). SE Richfield
			Trumbull County					
35-78-01	Newton	East Branch, Mahoning River	Newton Falls	1+	117	1831	Town	1.2 SE jct OH5 on OH534 (E Broad St), then 0.1 left and right on Arlington St. Newton Falls
			Union County					
35-80-01	Allen	Big Darby Creek	Upper Darby/ Potstersburg	1	94	1868	Partridge	1.7 E jct OH559 on OH245, then 1.6 left on Inskeep-Cratty Rd, then 0.1 right on North Lewisburg Rd (CR164). NE North Lewisburg
-02	Allen	Spain Creek	Spain Creek	1	64	c1870	Partridge	1.7 E jct OH559 on OH245, then 0.1 left on Cratty Rd (CR163). ENE Lewisburg
-03	Union	Treacle Creek	Winget Road/ Treacle Creek	1	94	1868	Partridge	2.1 E jct OH4 on OH161, then 1.2 left on Homer Rd (CR86) and 0.3 right on dead end Winget Rd (TR82). NE Irwin
-04	Union	Little Darby Creek	Bigelow/ Little Darby	1	102	1873	Partridge	2.0 W jct OH38 on OH161, then just right on Axe Handle Rd. (CR87). W Chuckery

Number	Township	Stream	Name	Spans	Length	Year	Type	Directions
Vinton County								
35-82-04	Jackson	Middle Fork, Salt Creek	Mt. Olive/ Grand Staff	1	48	1875	Queen	1.2 W jct OH683 on US50, then 1.5 right on CR18 and just right on TR8. NE Allensville
-05	Elk	pond	Bay/Tinker (closed)	1	63	1876	multiple King and arch (double)	1.5 N jct US50 on W side of OH93 in Junior Fairgrounds N edge McArthur
-06	Wilkesville	Raccoon	Geer Mill/ (closed) (bypassed)	3	165	1874	multiple King and arch (double)	0.1 SE jct OH124 on 2.8 right on CR8, 0.8 right on TR7 and 1.1 left on TR4 Sec14. SW Wilksville
-07	Vinton	Raccoon Creek	Eakins Mill/ Arbaugh (closed)	1	111	1870	multiple King and arch (double)	3.2 NE jct OH160 or 2.8 SW of OH689 on OH32 (Appalachian Highway), then 0.3 N on dead end CR38A. NE Radcliff
-10	Swan (M1992)	Brushy Fork Raccoon	Cox (closed) (bypassed)	1	40	1884	Queen	0.8 S jct OH56 on OH93, then 0.1 right on CR20. Creek N Creola
Washington County								
35-84-03	Palmer	West Branch, Wolf Creek	Shinn (closed)	1	98	1886	multiple King and arch	0.3 W of Wolf Creek intersection on OH676, then 2.6 left on TR91 and 0.2 left on TR447 Sec 14. SSW Wolf Creek
-06	Fairfield	West Branch, Little Hocking River	Henry (closed) (bypassed)	1	45	1894	multiple King	2.6 E jct OH555 on OH550, then 2.0 right on E side of bypassed section of TR61 Sec 20. SE Bartlett
-08	Decatur	West Branch, Little Hocking River	Root (closed) (bypassed)	1	65	1878	Long	7.3 NW jct US50/OH7 on OH555, then 0.4 right on E side of by passed section of CR6. N Decaturville
-11	Watertown	South Branch, Wolf Creek	Harra (closed) (bypassed	1	95	1878	Long	2.4 N jct OH676 on OH339, then 0.5 left on W side of bypassed section of TR172 NW Watertown
-12	Barlow	Southwest Fork, Wolf Creek	Bell	1	63	1888	multiple King	0.3 N jct OH550 on OH339, then 2.6 left on TR39 Sec 30 NNW Barlow
-17	Barlow (M1980)	brook	Mill Branch (closed)	1	59		multiple King	0.1 W jct OH339 on OH550, then 0.1 right in County Fairgrounds. At Barlow
-20	Marietta (M1994)	dry land	Schwenderman (closed) (private) (permission)	1	44	1894	multiple King	On Geoff/Kim Curran Farm. Several miles N Marietta on CR8.
-24	Newport	Little Muskingum River	Hills/Hildreth (closed) (bypassed)	1	122	1878	Howe	5.7 E jct OH7 on OH26, then 0.3 right on CR33. E. Marietta
-27	Lawrence	Little Muskingum River	Hune	1	128	1879	Long	7.4 SW jct OH260 on OH26, then 0.2 left on TR34 Sec 6. SW Bloomfield
-28	Ludlow	Little Muskingum River	Rinard (closed) (bypassed)	1	130	1876	Smith	4.0 SW jct OH260 on OH26, then just left on bypassed section of CR406. SW Bloomfield

Number	Township	Stream	Name	Spans	Length	Year	Type	Directions
			Williams County					
35-86-06	Lockport	Tiffen River	Lockport	3	176	1999	Howe	Near Lockport
			Wyandot County					
35-88-03	Crane (RB 1992)	Sandusky River	Parker	1	172	1873	Howe	4.5 NE jct OH53 on OH67, then 1.2 left on TR39 and 0.2 left on TR40 Sec 3. NNE Upper Sandusky
-05	Antrim (RB1994)	Sandusky River	Swartz	1	100	1878	Howe	2.2 E jct US23 on OH294, then 2.0 left on CR130. SE Upper Sandusky

OREGON
Benton County

Number	Township	Stream	Name	Spans	Length	Year	Type	Directions
37-02-04	Wren	Mary's River	Harris	1	75	c1929	Howe	0.1 right on OR223 from US20, right on Ritner Rd., right on Wren Rd. and 2.5 right on Harris Rd. (CR52).
-05	Alsea	Alsea River	Hayden	1	91	1918	Howe	1.7 W of main intersection in Alsea on OR34, then 0.1 left on Hayden Rd.
-09	Corvallis formerly NE Monroe (RB1989)	Willamette Slough	Irish Bend (foot)	1	60	1954	Howe	At Corvallis Lake, take US20/OR34 east, then right on 53rd St. and go into Corvallis Fairgrounds. Walk 0.5 right on bicycle path
			Coos County					
37-06-09	Remote	Sandy River	Sandy Creek	1	60	1921	Howe	14.0 ESE of Myrtle Point. N side of by passed section of OR42.
			Douglas County					
37-10-02	Drain (M1987)	Pass Creek	Krewson/Pass (foot)	1	61	1925	Howe	0.1 E jct OR38 on OR99 ("B" St), then 0.2 right on 2nd St. to S side of "A" St. in community park (behind Civic Center).
-04	Oakland	Calapooya Creek	Rochester	1	80	1933	Howe	1.5 NW jct I5 on OR138 (Exit 136), then 1.4 right and 0.5 left on CR10A (Stearns La.) NW Sutherlin
-06	Glide	Little River	Cavitt Creek	1	70	1943	Howe	1.2 S of OR138 and Glide on CR17A, then 6.7 left on Little River Rd (CR17) and just right on Cavitt Creek Rd (CR82A)
-07	Myrtle Creek	South Fork. Myrtle Creek	Neal Lane	1	42	1929	King	0.7 W jct I5 on OR99 (Main St) then 0.7 left on Riverside Dr (CR18A) and 0.4 right on Neal Lane Rd (CR124).
-14 formerly (-20-12)	Cottage Grove (M1990)	Myrtle Creek	Horse Creek	1	105	1930	Howe	Off OR99 in Mill Site Park.
			Jackson County					
37-15-02	Medford (M1987)	Little Butte Creek	Antelope Creek (foot)	1	58	1922	Queen	1.0 E of OR62 on N side of Main St (follow signs to Grist Mill at corner of Main and Royal Sts. At Eagle Point
-03	Lake Creek	Lost Creek	Lost Creek (closed) (foot)	1	39	1919	Queen	Turn off OR140E at sign for Lake Creek, go 4.9, then 0.4 right on W side of bypassed section of Lost Creek Rd.

Number	Township	Stream	Name	Spans	Length	Year	Type	Directions
			(cont'd) Jackson County					
-05	Wimer (RB1962)	Evans Creek	Wimer	1	85	1927	Queen double	8.0 N of I5 and Rogue River (Exit 48) on East Evans Creek Rd, then 0.5 right on Covered Bridge Rd.
-06	Ruch	Middle Fork, Applegate River	McKee (closed) (foot)	1	112	1917	Howe	2.7 S of OR238 and Ruch on Applegate Rd to Cameron then 5.8 right (ahead) on E side of bypassed section of Applegate Rd. At McKee
			Josephine County					
37-17-01	Sunny Valley	Grave Creek	Sunny Valley	1	105	1920	Howe	0.5 NE jct I5 on old Rte 99 (Exit 71).
			Lane County					
37-20-02	Crow	Coyote Creek	Coyote Creek/ Swing Log	1	60	1922	Howe	6.5 S of OR126 and Veneta on Territorial Highway (OR200), then 0.1 right on Battle Creek Rd. (CR4082). At Hadleyville
-04	Walton	Wildcat Creek	Wildcat	1	75	1925	Howe	12.0 E jct OR 36 on OR126 to Whitaker Creek/Clay Creek Recreation Area, then just right on Siuslaw Rd. and 0.2 right on Austa Rd. E Mapleton
-06	Greenleaf	Lake Creek	Lake Creek/ Nelson Creek	1	105	1928	Howe	17.0 NE jct OR126 on OR36 past Deadwood to milepost 17.5, then 0.2 right on Nelson Mountain Rd (CR3640) ENE Mapleton
-10	Vida (RB1987)	McKenzie River	Goodpasture	1	165	1938	Howe	21.0 E jct OR126BP and Springfield on OR126, then just right on Goodpasture Rd.
-11	McKenzie Bridge	McKenzie River	Belknap	1	120	1966	Howe	5.0 W jct OR 242 on OR126, then 1.0 left on McKenzie River Dr (old Rte 126) and just left. At Rainbow
-15	Jasper	Fall Creek	Pengra	1	120	1928	Howe	5.4 SE jct I5 on OR58 (Exit 188), then 2.5 left to Jasper, 4.0 right and 0.3 left on Jasper-Lowell Rd (CR220) and 0.1 right on Place Rd (CR6225).
-17	Lowell	Fall Creek	Unity	1	90	1936	Howe	15.0 SE jct I5 on OR58 (Exit 188), then 3.0 left on Jasper-Lowell Rd (CR6220).
-18	Lowell	Dexter Reservoir Middle Fork, Willamette River	Lowell (closed) (foot)	1	165	1945	Howe	15.0 SE jct I5 on OR58, then 0.1 left on W side of bypassed section of Jasper-Lowell Rd (CR6220).
-19	Dexter	Lost Creek	Parvin	1	75	1921	Howe	10.0 SE jct I5 on OR58 (Exit 188), then 4.0 right on Rattlesnake Creek Rd (CR6104), 0.2 right on Lost Valley Ln (CR6107) and just left on Parvin Rd (CR6122).

Number	Township	Stream	Name	Spans	Length	Year	Type	Directions
			(cont'd) Lane County					
-22	Cottage Grove	Row River (foot)	Currin (closed)	1	105	1925	Howe	3.2 E of I5 on Row River Rd (CR2400), then just right on bypassed section of Layng Rd. (CR542).
-23	Dorena	Row River (foot)	Dorena (closed)	1	105	1925	Howe	4.6 E of I5 on Row River Rd (CR2400), then 7.0 right on S side of bypassed section of Shore View Rd (CR2440).
-27	Cottage Grove	Mosby Creek	Mosby Creek	1	90	1920	Howe	0.9 E of OR 99 (9th St) on Main St, then 2.6 right on Mosby Creek Rd (CR2500) and 0.2 left on Layng Rd (CR2542)
-28	Cottage Grove	Mosby Creek	Stewart	1	60	1930	Howe	0.9 E of OR99 (9th St) on Main St., 3.6 right on Mosby Creek Rd, (CR2500) and 0.1 left on Garoutte Rd (CR2555).
-35	Marcola	Mohawk River	Earnest/ Russell	1	75	1938	Howe	2.1 NE of Wendling Rd (CR1975) and Marcola on Marcola Rd (CR1900), then Right on Pasche Rd. CR1980).
-36	Marcola	Mill Creek	Wendling	1	60	1938	Howe	On Wendling Rd, 3 NE Cre of Marcola
-38	Greenleaf (RB 1986)	Deadwood Creek	Deadwood	1	105	1932	Howe	5.0 N of OR36 and Deadwood on Deadwood Creek Rd., then 0.3 right on Deadwood Loop Rd.
-39	Westfir	North Fork of Middle Fork of Williamette River	Office	1	180	1944	Howe	2.5 E of OR38 and Deadwood (CR6128), then 0.2 left at Westfir Lumber Co.
-40	Cottage Grove	Coast Fork, Wilamette	Chambers Railroad (abandoned)	1	78	1936	Howe	0.5 W of OR99 (9th St) on Main St, then 0.3 left River on E side of South River Rd.
-41	Cottage	Coast Fork, Willamette River	Centennial (foot) (built of materials from -20-09 and -20-29)	1	84	1987	Howe	0.3 W of OR99 (9th St) on North Main St between 5th St and North River Rd.
			Lincoln County					
37-21-03	Chitwood (RB 1984)	Yaquina River	Chitwood	1	96	1930	Howe	15.5 E of Newport on US20 to just past milepost 18, then just right. E Toledo
-08	Yachats	North Fork, Yachats River	North Fk, Yachats River	1	42	1938	Howe	6.9 E of US101 and Yachats on Yachats River Rd, then 1.5 left on North Fork Rd (FS1484).
-11	Fisher	Five River	Fisher School (foot)	1	72	1919	Howe	10.0 SE of Tidewater on OR34, then 3.5 right on Fisher-Five Rivers Rd (FS141) to Denzer, 6.0 right to Fisher, ahead 0.7 and just right on bypassed section of Fisher School Rd. SSE Tidewater

Number	Township	Stream	Name	Spans	Length	Year	Type	Directions
\multicolumn{9}{c}{Linn County}							
37-22-02	Lyons	Thomas Creek	Hannah	1	105	1936	Howe	6.5 E of main intersection in Scio on OR226, then just right on Camp Morrison Rd (CR830). E Scio
-03	Scio	Thomas Creek	Shimanek	1	130	1966	Howe	2.3 E of main intersection in Scio on OR226, then 0.6 left on Gap Rd (CR604).
-04	Jefferson	Thomas Creek	Gilkey	1	120	1939	Howe	2.9 W of OR226 and Scio on Robinson Dr (CR630), Then 1.3 left on Goar Rd (CR629) WSW Scio
-05	Sweet Home	Thomas Creek	Weddle/ Devaney	1	130	1937	Howe	Rebuilt at Sweet Home in Sankey Park. (see -22-16) At Sweet Home
-06	Lacomb	Crabtree Creek	Larwod	1	105	1939	Howe	1.6 E of main intersection in Crabtree on OR226, then 6.3 right on Fish Hatchery Dr. (CR648). E Crabtree
-07	Scio	Crabtree Creek	Bohemian Hall/ Richardson Gap	1	130	1947	Howe	Stored at Linn County Maintenance Yard, 2.3 E of main intersection in Scio on OR226, then 0.1 right on W side of Richardson Gap Rd (CR669).
-08	Crabtree	Crabtree Creek	Hoffman	1	90	1936	Howe	2.3 E jct US20 on OR226, then 1.5 left on Hungary Hill Dr (CR647).
-09	Cascadia	South Santiam River	Short/ Cascadia	1	105	1945	Howe	1.0 W of town limit on US20, then 0.1 right on High Deck Rd.
-15	Crawfordsville	Calapooia River (foot)	Crawfordsville	1	105	1932	Howe	8.5 SW jct US20 on S side of by passed section of OR228.
-16	Jefferson	Ames Creek	Dahlenburg/ Holley Replica (foot)	1	20	1989	Howe	Just SW jct US20 (Main St) on OR228, then 0.1 left on Long St. 0.1 right on 12th Ave. and 0.2 left on Kalmia St. to Sankey Park Annex entrance. At Sweet Home
-17	Cascadia	South Santiam River	Cascadia State Park/	1	120	1928	Howe	38 E on US20 (exit 233) on deck from I5 to Cascadia State Park.
-19	Sweet Home (M1993)	Stone Brook	Joel Whittmore	1	20	1990	Howe	S of OR34, W of 1st St, at W entrance to town, in Clover Memorial Park
\multicolumn{9}{c}{Marion County}							
37-24-01	Silverton	Abiqua Creek	Gallon House	1	84	1916	Howe	1.3 N jct OR213 on OR214, then 0.5 left on Hobart Rd (CR649) and 0.5 right on Gallon House Rd. (CR647).
-02 formerly -22-01	Stayton (M1985) (RB 987)	Salem Power Canal	Jordan (closed) (foot) (burnt, only timbers remain)	1	90	1937	Howe	1.0 S of OR22 and Stayton/Sublimity turnoff on Stayton Rd, then 0.2 left to Pioneer Park entrance on S side of Marion St.

Number	Township	Stream	Name	Spans	Length	Year	Type	Directions
Polk County								
37-27-01	Pedee-Kings Valley (M1976)	Ritner Creek	Ritner Creek (closed)	1	75	1927	Howe	3.2 S of Pedee on E side of OR223 (0.6 N of Benton County line).
-03	Grand Ronde	South Yamhill River	Alva "Doc" Fourtner (private) (permission)	1	66	1932	Queen	1.8 W jct OR22 (west) on Grand Ronde Rd, 0.1 left on Ackerson Rd (CR688) to "Y" and left to last house.

PENNSYLVANIA
Adams County

Number	Township	Stream	Name	Spans	Length	Year	Type	Directions
38-01-01	Cumberland-Freedom	Marsh Creek	Saucks (closed)	1	102	1854	Town	1.0 SSW jct PA97 on Business US15, then 1.8 right on Pumping Station Rd (CR3005) and 0.2 left on Waterworks Rd (TR26). SW Gettysburg
-05	Latimore (M1994)	dry land	Reeser/Anderson Farm	1	79		Burr	5.5 N jct PA234 on PA194, then 1.0 left on Lake Meade Rd. (CR1012) and 1.8 left on W side of Stoney Point Rd. (CR1007). NNW East Berlin
-08	Hamilton-ban	Tom's Creek	Jack's Mountain/G. Donald McLaughlin	1	75	1892	Burr	2.9 N jct PA16 on PA116, then 0.5 left on Jack's Mountain Rd (CR3021). SW Fairfield
-14	Huntington-Tyrone	Bermudian Creek	Heike's (private)	1	64	1892	Burr	0.9 N jct PA234 on Business US15, then 1.5 left on Oxford Rd (CR1016) and 0.2 right on bypassed section of dead end TR585. NNW Heidlersburg

Bedford County

Number	Township	Stream	Name	Spans	Length	Year	Type	Directions
38-05-03	East	Brush Creek	Felton Mill (closed)	1	105	1892	Burr	0.4 W jct I70 on US30 (Exit 28) then 2.5 left and just left on bypassed section of CR2009. SW Breezewood
-11	Harrison-Napier	Raystown Branch, Juniata River	Heirline/Kinton	1	136	1902	Burr	1.0 N jct PA96 (south) on PA31, then 0.4 left on W W side of bypassed section of CR4007. N Mann's Choice
-12	Bedford (M1975)	Raystown Branch, Juniata River	Claycomb/Reynoldsdale (admission) (sidewalk added, 1975)	1	126	1884	Burr	1.8 N jct US330 on W side of Business 220 at entrance to Old Bedford Village.
-15	Hopewell	Yellow Creek	Hall's Mill	1	96	1872	Burr	1.0 E jct PA36 on PA26, then 0.5 left on CR4022 and just left on TR528. SE Edge Yellow Creek
-16	West St. Clair	Dunning Creek	Dr. Knisley (private)	1	87		Burr	1.0 E jct PA96 on PA56, then 0.2 right on W side of Chestnut Ridge Rd (CR4013) SE Pleasant
-17	West St. Clair	Dunning Creek	Ryot	1	81		Burr	2.5 S jct PA56 on PA96 to Ryot, then 0.4 left on TR559.

Number	Township	Stream	Name	Spans	Length	Year	Type	Directions
			(cont'd) Bedford County					
-18	Napier	Dunning Creek	Cuppert/ New Paris (closed) (private)	1	71		Burr	1.7 N CR4018 and main intersection in New Paris. On E side of PA96.
-19	Harrison	Raystown Branch, Juniata River	Diehl/ Turner	1	87	1892	Burr	1.9 W jct PA96, N on PA31, then 0.4 right on TR418. W Mann's Choice
-21	Londonderry	Gladden's Run	Fichtner/ Palo Alto	1	56	1880	multiple King	0.1 W of PA96 on S side of bypassed section of CR3002. W edge Palo Alto
-22	East St. Clair	Bob's Creek	Bowser/ Osterburg (closed)	1	98		Burr	3.1 NW jct US220 on PA869, then just left on bypassed section of TR575. WNW Osterburg
-23	East St. Clair	Dunning Creek	Snook's	1	81		Burr	1.4 SE jct PA96 on PA56, then 0.5 left on TR554 and just right on TR578. ESE Pleasantville
-24	Napir	Shawnee Creek	Colvin	1+	72		multiple King	0.2 W jct PA96 on US30, then 0.8 left on TR443. SW Schellsburg
-25	East Providence	Brush Creek	Jackson Mill (closed)	1	96	1889	Burr	Just W of I70 on CR2035 then 1.0 left on TR306, 1.0 right on TR409 and just left on TR412. SW Breezewood
-26	South-ampton	Town Creek	Hewitt	1	80	1879	Burr	3.3 N of MD State line on PA326 then 0.4 left on TR306 and 0.2 left on TR305. SE Hewitt
			Berks County					
38-06-01	Oley	Little Manatawny Creek	Pleasant-ville	1	139	1856	Burr	2.8 E jct PA662 on PA73, then 0.4 right on Covered Bridge Rd (CR1030). SE Pleasantville
-03	Oley	Manatawny Creek	Greisemer Mill	1	140	1832	Burr	0.2 N jct PA562 on PA662, then 2.6 right on Covered Bridge Rd (CR1030), 0.3 right and 0.2 left on TR579. NNE Yellow House
-05	Greenwich	Sacony Creek	Kutz Mill/ Sacony (cement floor)	1	106	1854	Burr	1.8 NW jct US222 on PA737, then 0.8 left on TR798. NW Kutztown
-06	Bern/	Tulpe-Spring Creek	Wertz/Red hocken	1 (closed)	218	1869	Burr	1.1 SSW jct PA183 on Van Reed Rd (West Reading) bypass), then then 0.8 left on Tulpehocken Creek Rd and just left on TR291. SE Leinbachs
-07	Greenwich/ Windsor	Maiden Creek	Dreibelbis Station	1	190	1869	Burr	2.4 S jct I78/US22 on PA143 (Exit 11), then just left on Balthasar Rd. S Lenhartsville

Number	Township	Stream	Name	Spans	Length	Year	Type	Directions
Bradford County								
38-08-01	Burlington	Brown's Creek	Knapp	1	95	1853	Burr	4.8 W jct US220 on US6 to Luther's Mills, then 0.1 right on Covered Bridge Rd. WNW Towanda
Bucks County								
38-09-02	Springfield	Durham Creek	Knecht/ Sleifer	1	110	1873	Town	1.0 S jct PA412 on PA212, then 1.3 left on Sleifer Valley Rd (CR4069) and 0.1 right.
-03	Solebury	Pidcock Creek	Van Sant	1	86	1875	Town	2.5 SE jct PA232 on PA32, then 1.5 right on Lurgan Rd (CR2101) and 0.6 right on TR392. S New Hope
-04	Tinicum	Roaring Rocks Creek	Erwinna	1	56	1871	Town	1.9 S of bridge to Frenchtown, NJ on PA32, then 0.3 right on CR1012 and 0.2 E on SR1014. W Erwinna
-05	Perkasie (M1958)	dry land	South Perkasie (closed)	1	98	1832	Town	3.0 E jct PA309 on PA152, then 0.2 left on W side of road in Lenape Park.
-06	East Rockhill/ Haycock	Tohickon Creek	Sheard Mill	1	130	1873	Town	2.4 NE jct PA313 on PA563, then 1.3 left on Old Bethlehem (CR4101), 0.6 left on Thatcher Rd (CR4043) and 0.3 left on SR4099. E Quakertown
-07	East Rockhill	East Branch, Perkomen Creek	Mood	1	126	1873	Town	1.4 N jct PA113 on PA152, then 1.5 right on Branch Rd and 0.2 left on CR4080. NE Perkasie
-08	Tinicum	Delaware Canal	Uhlerstown	2	110	1832	Town	Just S of bridge to Frenchtown, NJ on PA32, then 0.3 right on TR407. W edge Uhlerstown
-09	Tinicum	Tinicum Creek	Frankenfeld	2	136	1872	Town	3.3 S of bridge to Frenchtown, NJ on PA32, then 1.6 right on CR1013, 0.6 right and just right on Hollow Horn Rd. (TR440) W Tinicum
-10	Plumstead	Cabin Run Creek	Cabin Run	1	86	1874	Town	0.3 S of PA611 on PA413, then 1.4 left on Dark Hollow Rd. (CR1013) and 0.5 right on CR1011. E Pipersville
-11	Bedminster- Plumstead	Cabin Run Creek	Loux	1	90	1874	Town	0.3 S of PA611 on PA413, then 0.3 left on Dark Hollow Rd (CR1013) and 0.5 right on Carversville Rd (CR1003). E Pipersville
-12	New Britain	Pine Run	Iron Hill/ Pine Valley	1	81	1842	Town	2.0 W jct PA611 on US202, then 0.5 right on TR340. N New Britain
-13	Newtown	Neshaminy Creek	Twining Ford/ Schofield Ford	2	166	1997	Town and Queen	0.4 N jct PA332 on PA413, then 2.0 left on CR2036, and walk 0.3 W in Tyler State Park
-P1	Ralph Stover State Park	Tohickon Creek		2	179		Howe boxed pony	Just W of PA32 and Point Pleasant on CR1000, then 0.7 right on CR1010, 1.3 right on CR1009 and 0.2 right.

Number	Township	Stream	Name	Spans	Length	Year	Type	Directions
			Carbon County					
38-13-01	Franklin	dry land	Harrity/ Bucks (closed)	1	87	c1898	Howe	Just W jct PA9 (NE Turnpike on US209, then 0.1 right (CR2007) to Harrity, 3.0 right on CR2015 and 0.2 right at entrance to Beltzville State Park, 0.1 left and 0.6 left. NE Weissport
-02	Lower	Princess Creek	Little Gap	1	92		Burr	0.1 S jct CR2002/2004 (RB1986) and Little Gap.
			Chester County					
38-15-01	Elk/ New London	Big Elk Creek	Rudolph & Arthur	1	99	1986	Burr	1.5 W jct PA472 on PA841, then 0.1 left (ahead) on CR3005 and 0.4 left on Rudolph's Camp Rd (TR307) N Lewisville
-02	Elk	Little Elk Creek	Glen Hope	1	78	1889	Burr	1.3 SSE of PA472 and main intersection in Hickory Hill on Providence Rd (TR944), then 0.3 ahead.
-03	Elk/ New London	Big Elk Creek	Linton Stevens closed)	1	114	1886	Burr	0.4 E of main intersection in Hickory Hilll on PA472, then 0.8 left on TR344.
-05	West Marlborough	Buck Run	Speakman #1	1+	93	1881	Burr	1.1 N jct PA841 on PA82, then 0.3 right onTR371 and 0.1 left on CR3047. N Doe Run
-06	East Fallowfield	Buck Run (private)	Speakman #2 (twin) (permission)	1+	83	1881	Queen variation	1.1 SE jct PA841 on PA82, then just left on Apple Grove Rd (TR388), walk 0.8 N on McCorkle's Rd (former TR371) and 0.3 ahead through gate on left on farm road. E Doe Run
-07	East Fallowfield	Doe Run	Hayes Clark (twin) (private) (permission)	2	86	1971	Queen	Identical with -15-06 except 0.2 through gate on left. E Doe Run
-10	East and West Bradford	East Branch, Brandywine Creek	Gibson/ Harmony Hill	1	98	1872	Burr	2.5 S jct Business US30 on US322, then just left on Harmony Rd (TR391). S Downington
-11	Upper Uwchlan (M1971)	Branch of Marsh Creek	Larkin (closed)	1	60	1881	Burr	1.4 S jct PA401 on PA100, then 0.3 right on Font Rd, 1.7 left on Milford Rd (CR4045) and walk 0.2 S. N Downington
-12	East and West Vincent	French Creek	Hall/ Sheeder	1	120	1850	Burr	0.6 S jct PA23 on PA100, then 2.7 left on Pughtown Pughtown Rd. (CR1028) and 0.3 right on Sheeder Rd (CR1033). SE Bucktown
-13 #2	East and West Vincent	French Creek	Kennedy	1	120	1987	Burr	1.8 W jct PA23 on PA113, then 0.6 left through Kimberton and 0.4 ahead on Seven Stars Rd (TR522). N Kimbertown
-14	East Pikeland	French Creek	Rapp	1+	121	1866	Burr	1.4 NW jct PA113 on PA23, then 0.6 left on TR411 and 0.1 left on TR447. W Phoenixville

Number	Township	Stream	Name	Spans	Length	Year	Type	Directions
			(cont'd) Chester County					
-15	Valley Forge National Park	Valley Creek	Knox/ Valley Forge	1	66	1865	Burr	0.8 S of PA23 and E edge of Valley Forge on Valley Creek Rd, then just right. S Valley Forge
			Chester-Delaware Counties					
38-15-17	Newtown/ Willistown	Crum Creek	Bartram/ Goshen (closed)	1	80	1860	Burr	0.9 W jct PA252 on PA3, then 1.3 right on Boot Rd and just left on bypassed section of Goshen Rd (CR2020). W Newtown Square
			Chester-Lancaster Counties					
38-15-19 -36-38	West Fallowfield-Sadsbury	Octoraro Creek	Mercer	1	103	1860	Burr	1.6 W jct PA41 on PA372 to Christina, then 0.6 left on Noble Rd (CR2099), 0.5 Left on Creek Rd (TR455) And just left on Bailey's Crossroad Rd (TR332/TR976). S Atglen
-15 -22 -36-41	Lower Oxford-Little Britain (RB 1988)	Octoraro Creek	Pine Grove	2	200	1864	Burr	1.4 NW jct US1 on PA472, then 1.5 left on Street Rd (CR3028) and 0.2 right on CR3001.
			Clearfield County					
38-17-01	Bell	West Branch, Susquehanna River	McGee's Mills	1	116	1873	Burr	0.2 S jct PA36 on US219, then 0.3 left on TR322. At McGee's Mills
			Clinton County					
38-18-01	Logan	Big Fishing Creek	Logan Mill	1+	63	1874	Queen	4.7 W jct PA77 and Loganton On PA800, then 0.5 left on CR2007. E Tylersville
			Columbia County					
38-19-05 (M1986)	Briar Creek	Branch of Briar Creek	Fowlersville (closed)	1	40	1886	Queen	3.2 W jct US11 and Berwick on PA93, then 0.4 right on CR1011 and 0.4 right on access road to Briar Creek Park.
-06	Pine	Branch Run	Shoemaker	1	54	1881	Queen	1.0 N jct PA42 on PA442, then 0.1 left on CR4027. N Iola
-08	Greenwood-Pine	Little Fishing Creek	Sam Eckman	1	71	1876	Queen	1.3 N jct PA442 on PA42, then 2.4 right on CR4031 and 0.1 left on TR548. NE Sereno
-10	Fishing Creek	Huntington Creek	Josiah Hess/ Laubach	1	110	1875	Burr	4.0 N jct PA93 and Orangeville on PA487, then 1.4 right on CR1020 and 0.1 left on TR563 (bypassed section Of CR1020). E Forks
-11	Fishing Creek	Huntington Creek Overflow	East Paden (twin) (closed)	1	79	1850	Queen	4.0 NE jct PA93 and Orangeville on PA487, then 0.5 right on CR1020 and 0.1 right on TR565 (bypassed section of PA120). E Forks

Number	Township	Stream	Name	Spans	Length	Year	Type	Directions
			(cont'd) Columbia County					
-12	Fishing Creek	Huntington Creek (closed)	West Paden (twin)	1+	103	1850	Burr	Same as for -19-11
-14	Locust	Roaring Creek	Snyder	1	66	1876	Burr	3.5 SE jct PA487 on PA42, then 1.4 left on CR2001 and just left on TR361. ESE Slabtown
-15	formerly Slabtown (M1981)	Roaring Creek	Wagner	1	62	1856	Queen	Stored for rebuilding
-16	Cleveland	Roaring Creek	Davis	1	95	1875	Burr	2.6 SE jct PA487 on PA42, then 0.8 right on TR377 and just right on TR371. WNW Slabtown
-18	Hemlock/ Mt. Pleasant	Little Fishing Creek	Wanich	1	108	184	Burr	2.0 N jct I80 on PA42 (Exit 34), then 0.3 right on TR493 NNW Bloomsburg
-20	Cleveland	Roaring Creek	Esther Furnace	2	109	1882	Queen	3.5 SSE jct PA487 on PA42, then 1.8 right on TR375, 0.5 ahead on TR340 and 0.2 right on TR373. W Slabtown
-21	Fishing Creek	Fishing Creek	Stillwater	1	168	1849	Burr	2.1 S jct PA24 on PA487, then 0.1 left on TR629. At Stillwater
-23	Greenwood	Mud Run	Kramer	1	56	1881	Queen	0.7 S of PA2454 and main intersection in Rohrsburg on CR4041, then 0.5 right on TR595 and 0.2 left on TR572. SW Rohrsburg
-25	Jackson/ Pine	Little Fishing Creek	Jud Christian	1	60	1876	Queen	1.3 N jct PA442 on PA42, then 4.5 right on CR4031 and 0.1 right on Arden's Hill Rd. NE Sereno
-26	Orange	Green Creek	Patterson	1	82	1845	Burr	1.5 NNE jct PA93 on PA87, then 0.5 left on CR4020, 1.1 right on CR4041 and just left on TR575. N Orangeville
-29	Cleveland/ Franklin	Roaring Creek	Paar Mill	1	92	1865	Burr	2.9 SSW jct PA442 on PA87m then 0.3 left on CR3003 and 0.1 left onTR371. S Catawissa
-31	formerly Knoebel's Grove (M1986)	South Branch, Roaring Creek	Rohrbach	1	70	1846	Queen	Stored at Knoebel's Grove Amusement Park
-33	Montour	Fishing Creek	Rupert	1	185	1847	Burr	0.4 S jct US11 on PA42, then 0.3 left on CR4001 (old Rte 42), 0.1 left and 0.2 left on Reading St (TR449). NE edge Rupert
-34	Catawissa	Catawissa Creek	Hollingshead	1	128	1850	Burr	0.5 S jct PA487 on PA42/487, then 0.3 left on TR401, 0.4 left on Mountain Rd. (TR422) and just left on TR405.
-36	Jackson/ Pine	Little Fishing Creek	Creasyville	1	49	1881	Queen	1.9 W of main intersection in Waller on CR4031, then 1.1 left and 0.1 right on TR683. SW Waller

Number	Township	Stream	Name	Spans	Length	Year	Type	Directions

Number	Township	Stream	Name	Spans	Length	Year	Type	Directions
			(cont'd) Columbia County					
-37	Cleveland	Mugser Run	Johnson	1	66	1882	Queen	0.3 N of Northumberland County line on PA487, then 0.8 right (sharp) on TR318, 1.0 left on TR337 and 0.1 right on TR1320. ENE Elysburg
-46	Sugarloaf	dry land (private)	Paperdale	1	46		Queen	S side of Laubach Rd (TR816)
			Columbia-Northumberland Counties					
38-19-32 -49-12	Cleveland/ Rapho	South Branch, Roaring Creek	Krickbaum	1	68	1876	Queen	2.1 SE jct PA487 on PA54, then 0.6 left on TR354/TR459. N Bear Gap
-19-39 -49-13	Cleveland/ Rapho	South Branch, Roaring Creek	Lawrence L. Knoebel (private)	1	41	1875	Queen	3.0 ENE jct PA54 on E side of PA487 at Knoebel's Grove Campground. ESE Elysburg
-49 -49-07	Cleveland/ Rapho	South Branch, Roaring Creek	Richards	1	69	1875	Queen	1.9 NE jct PA54 on PA487, then 0.7 right on TR335/804. E Elysburg
			Cumberland County					
38-21-10	formerly W Newville (M1987)	Conodoguinet Creek	Thompson	1	165	1853	Burr	Stored at Laughlin Mill in Newville.
-11	Hopewell	Conodoguinet Creek	Ramp	1	128	1882	Burr	1.2 E jct PA696 on PA641, then 0.8 right on TR374. E. Newburg
			Cumberland-York Counties					
38-21-13	Upper Allen-Monaghan	Yellow Breeches Creek	Bowmansdale/Stoner (extensive alterations)	1	106	1867	Burr	1.0 SSE jct US15 on PA114, then 0.6 right on CR2004, 0.7 left on CR2026 and 0.3 left, on Messiah College Campus. S edge Grantham
			Dauphin County					
38-22-04	Washington	on bank of Wisconisco Creek	Wilhour Mill/ Saw Mill (abandoned) (to be moved to Collegeville, Montgomery Co.)	1	91		Burr	1.2 W jct PA225 on US209, then 1.0 right on W side of Municipal Rd (CR1007). NE Elizabethville
-05	Susquehanna formerly N. Harrisburg (M1940)	dry land	Everhart/ Fort Hunter (private)	1	36		King	Stored in 1980 for possible rebuilding.
-11	Washington	Wisconisco Creek	Henninger Farm/Stroup	1	72		Burr	2.2 E jct PA225 on US209, then 0.7 left on CR1006, 0.5 right on TR617 and 0.4 left on North Rd (TR624). NE Elizabethville
			Erie County					
38-25-02	Conneaut	West Branch, Conneaut Creek	Sherman/ Keepville	1	72	1873	multiple King	3.4 W jct PA18 on US6N, then 1.5 on Barney Rd (CR3003)
-03	Girard	Elk Creek	Gudgeonville	1	83	c1868	multiple King	0.2 W jct PA18 (north) on US20, then 1.8 right on Tannery Rd (CR3018) 0.8 right on Beckman Rd. (TR547) and 0.7 right on Gudgeonville Rd. (TR400)

Number	Township	Stream	Name	Spans	Length	Year	Type	Directions
			Erie County					
-04	Waterford	LeBoeuf Creek	Waterford	1	75	c1875	Town	0.4 E US19 on E 1st St, then 0.4 right on East St and 0.6 ahead on Niemeyer Rd. 0.7 (TR459).
			Franklin County					
38-28-01	Antrim	Conocheague Creek	Martin's Mill/ Shindle (closed)	2	225	1849	Town	1.7 W jct US11 on PA16, then 2.0 left on CR3005, 0.8 left and 1.1 left on TR341. SW Greencastle
-02	Montgomery	Licking Creek	Red/ Witherspoon	1	94	1883	Burr	1.2 NNW jct PA995 on PA416, then 0.7 right on TR328. N Welsh Run
			Greene County					
38-30-21	Cumberland	Muddy Creek	Carmichael	1	64	1889	Queen	0.1 E PA88 and main intersection on CR0021, then 0.2 left on Old Town Rd. and just left on N. Market St. N edge Carmichael
-24	Wayne	Hoover Run	King	1	56		Queen	2.3 N of main intersection in Brave on CR3013, then just left on TR371. N Brave.
-25	Morgan	Ruff Creek	Lippincott/ Cox Farm	1	32	1940	King	2.0 NW jct PA188 on PA21 then just left on TR568 WNW Lippincott
-26	Center	Pursley Creek	Nettie Wood	1	45	1882	Queen	3.0 WSW jct US19 and Waynesburg on PA18/21, then 1.8 left on CR3013 and just right on TR487. N Oak Forest
-28	Center	South Fork, Tenmile Creek	Scott	1	48	1885	Queen	2.9 WNW jct PA18, on PA21, then just left on TR424. W Rogersville
-29	Center	Hargus Creek	Shriver	1	46	1900	Queen	0.5 S jct PA21 on PA18, then 1.1 left on CR3011 and just left on TR454. S Rogersville
-30	Greene	Whiteley Creek	White	1	70	1919	Queen	1.2 E of I79 on CR2018 (Exit 2) then 0.6 right on CR2011 and 0.2 right on CR8009. W Garards Fort
			Huntingdon County					
38-31-01	Cromwell	Shade Creek	St. Mary/ Shade Gap	1	65	1889	Howe	2.5 NNW jct PA641 on PA522 Then just right on TR358. NNW Shade Gap
			Indiana County					
38-32-03	Washington	South Branch, Plum Creek	Trusal/ Dice	1	35	1870	Town	1.1 E of PA954 and E edge Willet on CR4006, then 0.2 right on TR406.
-04	Washington	South Branch, Plum Creek	Harmon	1	41	1910	Town	1.6 E of PA954 and E edge Willett on CR4006 then 0.2 right on bypassed section of TR488.
-05	Rayne	Crooked Creek	Kintersburg (closed)	1	62	1877	Howe	1.1 S jct PA85 on US119, then 1.4 left on CR1005 and just right on bypassed section of TR612. SE Home

Number	Township	Stream	Name	Spans	Length	Year	Type	Directions
			Indiana County					
-06	Armstrong	Crooked Creek	Thomas	1	88	1879	Town	1.8 E jct PA156 on US422, then 0.6 left on CR4001, 1.9 right on CR4002 and 0.1 right on TR414. E Selocta
			Jefferson County					
38-33-03	Warsaw	Wakefield Creek	McCracken (private)	1	26	1975	King	0.4 W of CR4005 and S edge Richardsville on S side of Howe Rd at Wakefield Springs Farm.
			Juniata County					
38-34-01	Beale/ Spruce Hill	Tuscarora Creek	Academia/ Pomeroy (closed)	2	279	1901	Burr	2.3 WSW jct PA74 on PA75, then 2.0 right and just right on TR349 (bypassed section of CR30150) SE edge Academia
-02	Greenwood	Cocolamus Creek	Dimmsville (closed)	1	108		Burr	5.8 E jct PA333 on PA235, then 1.2 right on W side of bypassed section of CR2017. W Seven Stars
-04	Milford	Licking Creek	Lehman/ Port Royal (private) (no truss members)	2	120	1888	stringer	0.2 N jct PA75 on PA333, then 0.1 left and just right on TR451. (bypassed section of CR3010). W edge Port Royal
			Juniata-Snyder Counties					
38-34-05 -55-05	Perry / Susquehanna (RB1987)	Mahantango Creek	Oriental/ Curry's Corner	1	69		multiple King	1.0 N jct US11/15 on PA104, then 3.0 left on CR2026 to Oriental and 2.0 right on CR2023. W Meiserville
-34-06	Perry/ Susquehanna	Mahantango Creek	Meiser's Mill Shaeffer	1	90	1907	Burr	1.0 N jct US11/15 on PA104, then 3.0 left on CR2026, 0.3 right on CR2023, 0.4 right on CR2024 and just left on bypassed section of CR2024. SW Meiserville
			Lancaster County					
38-36-01	Caernarvon	Conestoga River	Pool Forge/ Wimer (closed) (private)	1	99	1859	Burr	0.2 W of Churchtown Rd. and Churchtown on PA23, then 0.2 left on E side of bypassed section of Pool Forge Rd. (CR1017). W Churchtown
-02	Caernarvon	Conestoga River	Weaver Mill/ White Hall	1	88	1879	Burr	0.7 N jct PA23 on PA625, then 1.4 right and 0.2 left on Weaverland Rd (TR773). N Goodville
-03	West Lampeter (M1974)	Mill Creek	Kurtz Mill/ Bear's Mill	1	97	1876	Burr	0.8 S jct PA324 on US222, then 1.7 left on Golf Rd and 0.1 right on Kiwanis Dr. in Greater Lancaster County Park. SE edge Lancaster
-04	West Earl	Conestoga River	Eberly/ Bitzer's Mill	1	99	1846	Burr	1.2 SE jct US222 on US322, then 1.6 right on Conestoga Creek Rd, 0.1 left on Pinetown Rd and just right on Cider Mill Rd. (CR1013). SE Ephrata
-05	Manheim/ Upper Leacock (RB1974)	Conestoga River	Pinetown	1	135	1867	Burr	0.6 S jct PA772 on PA272, then 0.3 left on Creek Rd and 0.1 left on TR620 SW Brownsville

Number	Township	Stream	Name	Spans	Length	Year	Type	Directions
			(cont'd) Lancaster County					
-06 #2	Manheim/ Upper Leacock	Conestoga River	Hunsecker Mill	1	181	1975	Burr	2.4 NE jct US30 BP on PA272, then 1.8 right on Hunsecker Rd. (CR1029-TR620). NE edge Lancaster
-10	Earl	Muddy Creek	Oberholtzer's Mill/Red Run	1	119	1866	Burr	2.2 W of PA897 and Fivepointsville (CR1046), then 0.6 left on bypassed section Red Run (CR1044). SE Reamstown
-12	East and West Cocalico	Cocalico Creek	Bucher's Mill	1	73	1892	Burr	0.5 SW of Church St. intersection in Reamstown on PA272, then 0.1 left on Creek Rd and just right on TR955. WSW Reamstown
-13	Ephrata	Cocalico Creek	Keller/ Rettew's Mill	1	74	1891	Burr	0.2 W of PA272 and Ephrata on Rothsville Rd (CR1018), then 0.2 right on Rettew's Mill Rd (TR656). N Akron
-14	Ephrata/ Warwick	Cocalico Creek	Rosehill/ Wenger	1	89	1849	Burr	1.0 SW jct PA772 and Brownstown on PA272, then 0.6 right on Rose Hill Rd. and just left on Log Cabin Rd (TR797). WNW Brownstown
-15	Warwick (M1965)	pond	Hess Mill/ Buck Hill Farm (closed)	1	59	1844	Burr	2.0 N jct PA722 on PA501, then 0.3 right at driveway. S Lititz
-16	East Hempfield	Little Conestoga Creek	Landis Mill	1	53	1878	King	0.2 W of US30 BP on Harrisburg Pike, then 0.3 right on Plaza Blvd and 0.1 left on Shreiner Station Rd (TR560) at W edge of Park City Mall. NW edge Lancaster
-18	Colerain/ Little Britain	West Branch, Octoraro Creek	White Rock Forge	1	113	1884	Burr	1.0 SW of PA472 and main intersection in Kirkwood on Maple Shade Rd. (TR357), then 0.8 left on Noble Rd (CR2009) and 1.2 left on White Rock Rd. (TR337). S Kirkwood
-20	Leacock/ Paradise	Pequea Creek	Leaman Place/ Eshelman Mill	2	114	1894	Burr	1.3 E of main intersection in Paradise on US30, then 0.5 left on Belmount Rd (TR684).
-21	Leacock/ Paradise	Pequea Creek	Herr Mill/ Soudersburg (closed) (private)	2	178	1885	Burr	2.0 W of main intersection in Paradise on US30, then 0.5 left on bypassed section of Ronks Rd (TR696).
-22	West Lampeter/ Strasburg	Pequea Creek	Neff Mill	1	103	1875	Burr	1.1 W jct PA896 on PA741 (Miller St) then 0.2 left (ahead) on CR2030, 0.2 right on Hager Rd and 1.0 left on Penn Grant Rd (TR559). W Strasburg
-23	Strasburg/ West Lampeter	Pequea Creek	Lime Valley	1	104	1871	Burr	3.3 SE jct PA272 on US22, then 0.3 left on Lime Valley Rd (CR2020) and 0.4 right on Breneman Rd (TR498). SE Willow Street

Number	Township	Stream	Name	Spans	Length	Year	Type	Directions
			(cont'd) Lancaster County					
-25	Martic/ Pequea (RB1987)	Pequea Creek	Baumgardner	1	116	1860	Burr	2.2 N of main intersection in Martic Forge on PA324 to Marticville, then 0.4 right on Frogtown Rd (TR415) and 0.4 left on Covered Bridge Rd (TR427). NE Martic Forge
-28	Rapho/ West Hempfield	Big Chikiswalunga (Chickies) Creek	Forry Mill	1	103	1869	Burr	3.3 E jct PA441 on PA23, then 0.1 left on TR359 and 0.1 left on Bridge Valley Rd (TR362). E Marietta
-30	East Hempfield/ Rapho	Big Chikiswalunga (Chickies) Creek	Shenck Mill	1	96	1855	Burr	0.6 E of PA283 on Spooky Nook Rd (CR8007), then 0.6 left on Shenck Rd (TR396) and just left on Erisman Rd (TR372). N Landisville
-31	Penn-Rapho (M1972)	Big Chikiswalunga (Chickies) Creek	Jacob Shearer (private)	1	89	1856	Burr	0.4 NE of PA72 on High St, then 0.3 left on Laurel St and 0.2 right at N end of Adele Ave in Veterans' Memorial Park E edge Manheim
-32	Rapho	Big Chikiswalunga (Chickies) Creek	Kauffman Distillery/ Sporting Hill	1	96	1874	Burr	1.4 SW jct PA72 on PA772, then 0.2 left on Sun Hill Rd (TR889). SW Manheim
-33	Bart (RB1985)	West Branch, Octoraro Creek	Jackson Sawmill	1	143	1878	Burr	1.5 W jct PA896 on PA372, then 1.7 left on Mount Pleasant Rd (TR696). S Georgetown
-34	Clay/ Warwick	Hammer Creek	Erb's	1	80	1887	Burr	2.4 W jct PA272 on PA772, then 0.8 right on Picnic Woods Rd and 0.4 right on Erb's Bridge Rd (TR634). N Millway
-36	Manheim	Little Chikiswalunga (Chickies) Creek	Risser Mill/ Horst Mill	1	82	1849	Burr	0.1 W jct PA772 (north) on PA230, then 0.8 right on Fairview St (CR4075), 1.4 right on Risser Mill Rd (TR350) and just right on Mount Pleasant Rd (CR4010). Mount Joy
-37	Rapho/ West Hempfield	Big Chikiswalunga (Chickies) Creek	Seigrist Mill	1	102	1885	Burr	3.9 E of PA441 on PA23, then 0.6 left on Farmdale Rd (CR4001) and 0.4 left on Seigrist Rd (TR360). ENE Marietta
-43	East Lampeter	Branch of Mill Creek Creek	Willows (private) (built of materials from -36-24 and -36-27)	1	73	1962	Burr	0.1 W jct PA896 on N side of US30 (beside Amish Farm Exhibit). E Lancaster
-57	Conestoga-Martic	Pequea Creek	Colemanville/ Martic Forge (replaced -36-26, moved 75 ft downstream and raised 5 ft)	1	167	1990	Burr	0.1 W of main intersection in Martic Forge on PA324, then 0.2 left on Fox Hollow Rd (TR408). W Martic Forge

Number	Township	Stream	Name	Spans	Length	Year	Type	Directions
			Lawrence County					
38-37-01	Slippery Rock	Slippery Rock	McConnell's Mill	1	101	1874	Howe	0.3 W jct US129 on US422, then 0.7 left on TR526, 0.5 left (ahead) on access road to McConnell's Mill State Park (TR415), 0.2 right and 0.1 left. SSE Rose Point
-02	Wilmington	Neshannock River	Banks	1	129	1889	Burr	1.4 NW jct PA168 on PA956, then 0.2 right on Covered Bridge Rd (TR476) NE Neashannock Falls
			Lehigh County					
38-39-01	Allentown-Salisbury	Little Lehigh Creek	Bogert	1+	169	1841	Burr	0.4 S jct PA309 on PA29, then 1.1 left on Hatchery Rd (CR2010) and 0.1 left on E side of bypassed section of Oxford Dr (CR2007) in Little Lehigh Park. SW edge Allentown
-02	South Whitehall	Jordan Creek	Wehr	1+	138	1841	Burr	0.5 S of Kernsville Rd and Orefield on PA309, then 0.6 left on Parkland Terrace Rd (TR593) and 0.2 left on Wehr Mill Rd (TR597).
-03	South Whitehall	Jordan Creek	Manassas	1	129	1858	Burr	1.1 E of PA309 on Orefield Rd (CR4003), then 0.2 left and 0.6 right on Lapp Rd (TR602). E Orefield
-04	North Whitehal	Jordan Creek	Rex	1	139	1858	Burr	1.2 W on PA309 and Orefield on Kernsville Rd (CR4008) then 0.5 right on Jordan Rd. (TR593). W Orefield
-05	North Whitehall	Jordan Creek	Geiger	1	130	1858	Burr	1.2 W on PA309 and Orefield- Kernsville Rd (TR593), then 1.5 right on Jordan Rd (TR593), 0.4 right (ahead) on TR582 and 0.2 right on Old Packhouse Rd (TR681). WNW Orefield
-06	North Whitehall	Jordan Creek	Schlicher	1	117	1882	Burr	0.2 SE jct PA873 on PA309, then 1.3 right on Trexler Game Preserve Rd (CR4007). SW Schnecksvill
			Luzerne County					
38-40-01	Huntington	Huntington Creek	Bittenbender (private)	1+	76	1882	Queen	0.9 S of PA239 and Huntington Mills on E side of CR4006 S Huntington Mills
			Lycoming County					
38-41-01	Jackson	Blockhouse Creek	Buttonwood	1	69	1898	multiple King variation	1.1 NE of PA284 on old Rte 15 (CR1009), then 0.5 left on TR816. N Buttonwood
-02	Cogan House	Larry's Creek	Cogan House/ Buckhorn	1	90	1877	Burr	2.5 ENE jct PA287 on PA1 PA184 then 1.4 right on TR786 and just ahead on dead end TR784. E Brookside

Number	Township	Stream	Name	Spans	Length	Year	Type	Directions
			(cont'd) Lycoming County					
-03	Moreland	Little Muncy Creek	Fraser/ Moreland	1	85	1888	Burr	1.4 S of main intersection (CR2015) in Lairdsville on PA118, then 0.9 left on CR2060 and 0.3 left. SW Lairdsville
			Mercer County					
38-43-01	Pymatuning	Shenango River	Kidd's Mill (closed)	1	124	1869	Smith	0.8 S jct PA358, 3.0 right on Hamburg Rd, 0.2 right and 0.1 left on bypassed section of Kidd's Mill Rd (CR4012). S Shenango
			Montour County					
38-47-03	Liberty	Chillis- quaque Creek	Old Keefer	1	80	1853	Burr	0.4 W jct PA54 on PA254, then 0.7 left on CR3012 and 0.3 left on TR346. SW Washingtonville
			Montour-Northumberland Counties					
38-47-01	Liberty/ East Chillis- quaque	Chillis- quaque Creek	Sam Wagner/ Gottlieb Brown	1	95	1881	Burr	3.1 ESE jct PA147 on PA642, then 0.7 left on CR1029 and just right on CR3013/1020. ESE Milton
			Northampton County					
38-48-01	Allen	Hoken- dauqua Creek	Solt's Mill/ Kreisersville (closed)	1	115	1840	Burr	0.2 E of Lehigh County line on PA329, then 2.5 left and 0.1 right on bypassed section of Kreisersville Rd (CR4003). N Northampton
			Northumberland County					
38-49-02	Upper Augusta	Shamokin Creek	Keefer Station	1	97	1888	Burr	0.4 E jct PAS890 on PA61, then 0.5 left on CR4011, 1.8 left ahead) on TR509 and 0.4 left on TR698. E Sunbury
-05	East and West Chillis- quque	Chillis- quaque Creek	Rishel	1	121	1830	Burr	1.0 E jct PA147 on PA45, then 0.4 right on TR576 and 0.6 left on TR573. NE Chillisquaque
-06 #2	Washington	Schwaben Creek	Rebuck/ Himmel	1	43	1983	multiple King	3.5 NE jct PA147 on PA225, then 2.8 E on CR3010 and 0.3 left to end of TR442. ENE Herndon
-07	Point	brook	Mertz (private)	2	47	1976	multiple King	2.5 NW jct US11 on PA147, then 0.5 right on CR1024 and 0.3 left and just right on Mirkwood Rd. NW Northumberland
			Perry County					
38-50-03	Southwest Madison	Sherman's Creek	Flickinger Mill/ Bistline	1+	100	1871	Burr	2.7 ENE jct PA17 and Blain on CR274, then 1.2 right on CR3005. S Andersonburg
-04	Southeast	Sherman's Creek	Cisna Mill/ Adair	2+	176	1884	Burr	2.7 W jct PA850 on PA274, then 0.4 left on Couchtown Rd (CR3008). E Andersonburg
-06	Liverpool	Wildcat Creek	Red (closed)	1	55	1886	Burr variation	0.3 S of PA17/235 on US11/15, then 1.1 right on CR1010 and 0.2 right on E side of bypassed section of CR1005. W Liverpool

Number	Township	Stream	Name	Spans	Length	Year	Type	Directions
			(cont'd) Perry County					
-07	Saville	Big Buffalo Creek	Saville	1	73	1903	Burr	0.3 SW jct PA74 on PA17, then 2.6 right on Saville Rd (CR4002) and just left on CR4001.
-09	Saville	Big Buffalo Creek	Kochenderfer (closed)	1	71	1919	Burr variation	3.0 SW jct PA74 and Ickesburg on PA17, then 0.3 left on E side of bypassed section of Fitz Creek Rd, (TR332).
-10	Tyrone	Sherman's Creek	Landisburg/ Rice	2	132	1869	Burr	0.1 S jct PA233 on PA850, then 0.4 right on Kennedy Valley Rd (TR333). SSW Landisburg
-11	Toboyne	Sherman's Creek	New Germantown	1+	74	1891	Burr variation	3.6 WSW jct PA17 and Blain on PA274, then 0.2 left on TR302. SE edge New Germantown
-12	Jackson	Sherman's Creek	Mount Pleasant	1	73	1918	Burr variation	3.1 WSW jct PA17 and Bla Blain on PA274, then 0.2 left on Mt. Pleasant Rd (TR304). WSW Blain
-13	Jackson	Sherman's Creek	Book/ Kaufman	1	88	1884	Burr	1.1 WSW jct PA17 on PA274 then 0.3 left on Three Springs Rd (CR3003). SW Blain
-14	Jackson	Sherman's Creek	Enslow/ Turkey Tail	1+	117	1904	Burr	0.3 SE jct PA17 on PA274, then 0.9 right on CR3006 and 0.2 left on Adam's Grove Rd (TR312). SE Blain
-15	Northeast Madison/ Tyrone	Bixler Run	Wagoner's Mill/ Thompson	1	86	1889	Burr	1.3 W jct PA274/850 on combined routes, then 0.2 left on old section of TR579. W Loysville
-16	Wheatfield	Sherman's Creek	Dellville	2	175	1889	Burr	2.2 SSE jct PA34/274 and Meck's Corner on Dellville Rd (CR2002), then on Pine Hill Rd (TR456). Dellville
-17	Oliver	Big Buffalo Creek	Fleisher	2	125	1887	Burr	0.7 N jct PA34 on PA849 (W), then 0.4 right (ahead) on CR1024 and 1.0 left on dead end Fairground Rd (TR477). NW Newport
-18	Centre/ Juniata (M1970)	Little Buffalo Creek	Clay/ Wahneta	1	81	1890	Burr	0.3 SW jct PA849 (east) on PA34, then 1.6 right on Little Buffalo Creek Rd (CR4010), 0.2 left and 0.1 right in Little Buffalo State Park. SW Newport
			Philadelphia County					
38-51-01	Philadelphia	Wissahickon Creek	Thomas Mill (closed)	1	97	1855	Howe	0.5 SSW of US422 (Germantown Ave) and Chestnut Hill Hospital on Chestnut Hill Ave, then walk 0.6 right on Thomas Mill Rd. in Fairmount Park. NW Section Philadelphia

Number	Township	Stream	Name	Spans	Length	Year	Type	Directions
			Schuylkill County					
38-54-01	Washington	Little Swatara Creek	Zimmerman	1	65	c1880	Burr	3.0 E jct PA501 on PA895, then 0.2 right on TR661. E Pine Grove
-02	Washington	Little Swatara Creek	Rock	1	56	1870	Burr	4.7 E jct PA501 on PA895, then 0.2 left on Lover's Creek Rd (TR452). E Pine Grove
			Snyder County					
38-55-02	Beaver	Middle Creek	Beavertown/ Dreese (closed)	1	100	c1870	Burr	2.6 E of main intersection in Beavertown on US522, then 0.9 left on bypassed section of Covered Bridge Rd (TR600).
-03	Spring (M1981)	Middle Creek	Klinepeter/ Overflow	1	102	1871	Burr	0.2 W jct PA235 on Beaver Springs US522, then 0.1 left on Railroad Ave (TR427)
-04	Perry	North Branch, Mahantango Creek	Aline/ Meiserville (closed)	1	67	1884	Burr	2.6 N of Juniata County line on PA104, then just left on bypassed section of Zimmerman Rd (TR335). N Meiserville
			Somerset County					
38-56-01	Brother's Valley	Buffalo Creek	Burkholder/ Beechdale	1	52	1870	Burr	2.2 NE jct PA650 on US219, then 0.1 left on TR548. NE Garrett
-02	Fairhope	Brush Creek	Packsaddle/ Doc Miller	1	48	1870	multiple King	4.3 NW of main intersection in Fairhope on CR2019, then 0.2 left on TR772 and 0.2 left on TR407.
-03	Middle Creek	Laurel Hill Creek	Barronvale (closed) (private)	2	162	1902	Burr	2.0 W jct PA281 on PA253, then 1.0 right, 0.1 right and just left on bypassed section of CR3035. NW New Lexington
-05	Lincoln (M1961)	Haupt Run	Cox Creek/ Roberts (closed)	1	61	1859	Burr	0.1 N jct PA601 to entrance to Haupt Museum on side of PA985. N Somerset
-06	Middle Creek	Laurel Hill Creek	King (closed) (private)	1+	120	1906	Burr	1.8 W jct PA281 on S side of bypassed section of PA653. SW Somerset
-08	Stony Creek	Stony Creek	Glessner	1+	96	1880	Burr	0.8 NNW of main intersection in Shanksville on CR1007, then 0.4 left on TR565. NW Shanksville
-09	Allegheny	Raystown Branch, Juniata	New Baltimore	1+	86	1879	multiple King	0.9 W of Bedford County line on CR1015, then just right on TR812. NE edge River New Baltimore
-10	Quema-honing	Stony Creek	Trostletown/ Kantner	2+	113	1845	multiple King and Queen Variation	0.3 E jct PA281 on US30, then 0.1 right and just right in Lion's Club Park. S edge Stoyestow S edge Stoyestow
-11	Conemaugh	Ben's Creek	Shaffer/ Ben's Creek	1	67	1877	Burr	2.0 W jct PA403 on PA985, then just left on Covered Bridge Rd (TR634). SW edge Johnstown
-12	Lower Turkey Foot	Laurel Hill Creek	Lower Humbert/ Faidley	1	125	1891	Burr	1.0 NE of main intersection in Ursina on PA281, then 1.0 left on CR3007 and just left on dead end TR393.

Number	Township	Stream	Name	Spans	Length	Year	Type	Directions
Sullivan County								
38-57-01	Forks	Loyalsock Creek	Forksville	1	163	1850	Burr	0.2 S jct PA87 on PA154, then just right on CR4012. S edge Forksville
-02	Hillsgrove	Loyalsock Creek	Hillsgrove/ Rinkers	1	186	c1850	Burr	4.6 SW jct PA154 on PA87, then just right on TR359 and 0.2 left on PA357. SW Forksville
-03	Davidson	Muncy Creek	Davidson/ Sonestown	1	110	c1850	Burr	1.7 E jct PA42 on US220, then just right on Robins Rd (TR310). E Muncy Valley
Susquehanna County								
38—58-01	New Milford (M1965 stream from Delaware County, NY)	unnamed	L.C. Beavan/ Old Mill Village (built from one truss of original bridge)	1	29	1850	Town	0.9 S jct US11 on PA848 to entrance on E side of private road.
Union County								
38-60-01	Hartley	Penn's Creek	Millmont/ Glen Iron	1	154	1855	Burr	3.0 E of PA235 and Glen Iron on Penn's Creek Rd (CR3004) and just right on Covered Bridge Rd.
-02	West Buffalo	Buffalo Creek	Hayes	1	70	1882	multiple King	2.0 W jct PA104 on PA45, 0.6 right on Hoover Rd (TR376). W Mifflinburg
-03	West Buffalo (RB1959)	Buffalo Creek	Hassenplug (steel floor)	1	71	c1825	Burr	0.4 N jct PA45/304 on N 45th St. N edge Mifflinburg
-04	White Deer	White Deer Creek	Factory/ Horsham	1	60	1880	Burr variation	1.6 W of US15 on White Deer Pike (CR1010) (White Deer Exit), then 0.2 left on TR516. NNW West Milton
-05	Kelly	Little Buffalo Creek	Hubler/ Lewisburg (closed) (permission)	1	33	1850	multiple King	1.7 W jct US15 on PA192, then 1.6 right on Strawbridge Rd. to N end of Buffalo Creek. Bridge is on a private road. Walk on driveway. (E end of bridge is on penitentiary grounds). NW Lewisburg
-06	Lewisburg Huffnagle	Bull Run	Gordon (foot)	1	46	1981	Town	0.3 E jct US15, on N side of PA45 at 6th St.
Washington County								
38-63-03	East Finley	Rocky Run	Sprowl	1+	36	1875	King	1.5 SE of PA23 and East Finley on CR3035 then just left on TR450.
-08	Amwell	Tenmile Fork of Wheeling Creek	Bailey	1+	71	1889	Burr	1.4 S of main intersection in Amity on US19, then 0.5 left on CR2020 and 0.2 right on TR636. SSE Amity
-09	East Finley	Templeton Fork of Enlow's Fork, Wheeling Creek	Brownlee/ Stout	1+	41		King	2.1 N of main intersection in East Finley on PA23, then 0.2 left on TR450 and just right on TR414.

Number	Township	Stream	Name	Spans	Length	Year	Type	Directions
		(cont'd) Washington County						
-10	West Finley	Robinson Fork of Enlow's Fork, Wheeling Creek	Crawford	1+	49		Queen	0.7 NW of CR4028 and West Finley on CR3037, then just left on TR307.
-11	West Finley	Robinson Run	Danley	1+	48		Queen	1.2 N of CR3026 and Good Intent on CR3028, then just right on TR379. N Good Intent
-12	Morris	Short Creek	Day	1	41	c1875	Queen	1.0 SW jct PA221 on PA18, then just left on TR339. S Prosperity
-13	Hanover (M1987)	ravine	Devil's Den/ McClurg	1	31		King	0.7 W of PA18 to entrance to Township Park on S side of old Rte 22 (CR4004) opposite Hanover Township Building. W edge Florence
-14	Nottingham (M1975)	Branch of Mingo	Ebenezer Church Creek	1+	38		Queen	0.8 NE of PA136 and Kammerer, then 0.4 right on Mingo Creek Park Rd. and 0.1 right in Mingo Creek County Park.
-15	West Finley	Middle Branch, Wheeling Creek	Erskine	1+	48	1845	Queen	2.3 S I70 on CR3023 (Exit 1) then 0.6 right on CR3018, and just left on TR314. S West Alexander
-16	Nottingham	Mingo Creek	Henry	1	41	c1881	Queen	0.7 W jct PA917 on PA136, then 0.5 right on TR822. NW Ginger Hill
-17	Amwell	Tenmile Creek	Hughes	1	64	1889	Queen	Just E of I79 on Ten Mile Rd (CR2020) (Exit 5), then 0.2 left on bypassed section of TR688. W Ten Mile
-18	Hanover	King's Creek	Jackson's Mill	1+	46		Queen	0.7 E of WV State line on old Rte 22 (CR4004), then 1.9 left on on TR853. NNE Paris
-19	Mount Pleasant	Raccoon Creek	Krepp's	1+	30		King	2.1 SW of main intersection in Cherry Valley on CR4015, then just left on TR799.
-20	North	South Bethlehem Pigeon Creek	Leatherman Branch,	1+	44		Queen	2.5 SE jct PA519 on US40, then 1.3 left on TR445 and 0.7 left on TR449. NW Cokeburg.
-21	Hanover	Brush Run	Lyle	1	37		Queen	0.2 N of old Rte 122 on PA18, then 2.5 right on Five Point's Rd. and 2.4 right on TR861. ENE Florence
-22	West Finley	Templeton Fork of Enlow's Fork, Wheeling Creek	Longdon/ Miller	1+	77		Queen	2.3 SSE CR3029 and West Finley on CR3037, then 0.6 left on CR4016/3026 and 0.3 left on TR414.
-23	Donegal	Branch of Middle Wheeling Creek	Blaney/May	1+	40	1882	Queen	0.4 N of I70 on CR3023 (Exit 1), then 0.4 right TR903 and 1.4 right on TR423. SE West Alexander
-26	East Finley	Templeton Fork of Enlow's Fork, Wheeling Creek	Plant	1	34	1876	King	1.2 SW of PA231 and East Finley on CR3035, then 0.1 right on TR450 and 1.0 left (ahead) on TR408. Caution: steep hill

Number	Township	Stream	Name	Spans	Length	Year	Type	Directions
			(cont'd) Washington County					
-27	Hanover	Aunt Clara's Fork, King's Creek	Freeman/ Ralston (private)	1	34	1915	King	0.4 E of WV State line on old Rte 22 (PA404), then 3.4 left on PA346 and 0.5 dead end TR352. N Paris
-28	Cross Creek/ Hopewell (M1978)	Cross Creek	Wilson's Mill	1	40	1889	King	1.5 W jct PA18 on PA50 to Woodrow, then 1.9 on TR486 to Cross Creek County Park. NE West Middletown
-29	East Finley (M1998)	Robinson Run	Wyit Sprowls	1+	52		Queen	In E. Finley Park
-30	Somerset	North Branch, Pigeon Creek	Wright/Cerl	1+	24		King	Just N of I70 McIlvaine Rd. (CR8026) (Exit 10), then 1.4 left on TR647 and 0.3 left on Sumney Rd (TR802). NW Bentleyville
-33	Hanover	Harmon Creek	Doc Hanlin (lying in creek)	1	15	1870	King	1.3 left jct PA18 on old US22, 1.2 left on unnamed dirt road. S Florence
-34	Blaine	Buffalo Creek	Sawhill	1	57	1915	Queen	2.9 SE jct PA331 on PA221, then just right on TR426. NW Taylorsville
-35 formerly -30-06	Jefferson	ravine	Pine Bank/ Meadowcroft Village (private) (admission)	1	39	1870	King	Just N of PA50 and Avella on CR4029, then 3.5 left on Penowa Rd (CR4018) in Meadowcroft Village
			Westmoreland County					
38-65-01	Sewickley/ West Huntingdon (RB1988)	Sewickley Creek	Bell's Mills	1	107	1859	Burr	2.4 ENE of PA31 on PA136, then 0.5 right on CR3012 and just right on CR3061. E West Newton

RHODE ISLAND
Providence County

Number	Township	Stream	Name	Spans	Length	Year	Type	Directions
39-05-01	Foster	Hemlock Brook	Swamp Meadow (not true Truss)	1	36	1992	Town	1.1 S jct US6 on RI94 and 0.1 right on Central Pike. Pike.

SOUTH CAROLINA
Greenville County

Number	Township	Stream	Name	Spans	Length	Year	Type	Directions
40-23-02	Gowensville RB1992	Beaver Dam Creek	Campbell (closed)	1	41	1909	Howe	0.8 W jct SC14 on SC414, then 0.5 left on Pleasant Hill Rd and 0.1 right on bypassed section of Campbell Bridge Rd.

TENNESSEE
Carter County

Number	Township	Stream	Name	Spans	Length	Year	Type	Directions
42-10-01	Elizabethton	Doe River	Elizabethton	1	134	1882	Howe	0.2 S jct TN91 on US19E/321, then 0.1 right On Elk Ave, 0.1 left on Main St and 0.1 right on 3rd St between Main St and Riverside Dr.

Dyer County

Number	Township	Stream	Name	Spans	Length	Year	Type	Directions
42-23-01	Trimble (M1997)	dry land	Emerson E. Parks Farm	1	33	1910	King	In Trimble at the N end of Parks Plaza (Main St. extension) In Park.

Number	Township	Stream	Name	Spans	Length	Year	Type	Directions
			Greene County					
42-30-01	Warrensburg	Little Chucky Creek	Bible/Chucky	1	57	1922	Queen	Go 7.0 SW from Greeneville on Warrensburg Rd (US349/CR705), and just right on bypassed section of Denver Bible Rd.
			Hamblen County					
42-32-01	North	Knox Brook	Clifford Holder	2	27	1919	stringer	0.5 N jct US11E on US25E, then 5.5 left on Cherokee Rd, and just left.
			Montgomery County					
42-63-01	Port Royal	Red River	Port Royal	2	180	1977	Howe	3.4 E from exit 11 of I24 on TN76, then left on Old Clarksville-Springfield Rd to end of TN238. In Port Royal State Park
			Obion County					
42-66-01	Trimble	Obion River Drainage Drainage Canal	Parks Farm (private) (two covered approach spans)	1	61	1910	King variation	0.5 N jct TN105 on US51/TN3 then 0.2 left on farm access road.
			Sevier County					
-01	Harrisburg	East Fork, Little Pigeon River	Pigeon River	1+	64	1875	Queen	4.2 E jct TN66 on US411, 0.9 right on TN334, right on Harrisburg Rd. and just right.

TEXAS
Nacadoches County

Number	Township	Stream	Name	Spans	Length	Year	Type	Directions
43-203-01	DeSoto	Spring off Spears Creek	Winnie's	1	36	1992	Town	26 E on TX103 from Lufkin, then 1.5 left on TX1277 to 1341 Winding Brook at Hensarling Ranch

VERMONT
Addison County

Number	Township	Stream	Name	Spans	Length	Year	Type	Directions
45-01-01	Cornwall	Otter Creek	Station/Salisbury/Creek Road/Cedar Swam	1+	155	1865	Town	3.2 S jct VT74 on VT30, then 1.8 left on Swamp Rd at Cornwall town line.
-02	Ferrisburg (M1958)	pond	Old Hollow/Old Covered Bridge Farm (private)	1	85	1850s	Town	2.9 N jct VT22A on W side of US7.
-03	Middlebury-New Haven	Muddy Branch, New Haven River	Halpin/High	1	66	1824	Town	0.1 SE jct VT30 on US7, then 1.1 left on Washington St, then 1.5 left (ahead) on Halpin Rd and 0.3 right on dead end road.
-04	Middlebury-Weybridge	Otter Creek	Pulp Mill/Paper Mill (double)	1+	199	c1820	Burr	0.7 NW jct VT125 on VT23, then 0.5 right on Horse Rd and just right on Pulp Mill Bridge Rd.
-05	Shoreham	Lemon Fair River	East Shoreham Railroad/Rutland Railroad (closed)	1	109	1897	Howe	2.7 N jct VT73 (East) on VT30, then 2.8 left on Shoreham-Whiting Rd and 0.7 left on W side of abandoned right-of-way adjacent to East Shoreham Rd.

Bennington County

Number	Township	Stream	Name	Spans	Length	Year	Type	Directions
45-02-01	Arlington	Batten Kill	Bridge at the Green/Arlington Green	1	80	1852	Town	2.5 E NY State line on VT313, then just right on Covered Bridge Rd.

Number	Township	Stream	Name	Spans	Length	Year	Type	Directions
(cont'd) Bennington County								
-02	Bennington	Walloomsac River	Henry	1	121	c1840	Town	1.2 S jct VT67 on VT67A, then 0.5 right, and just left on River Rd.
-03 #2	Bennington	Walloomsac River	Papermill Village	1	131	2000	Town	1.2 NW jct US7 (Exit 1) on VT67A, then just left on bypassed section of Murphy Rd.
-04	Bennington	Walloomsac River	Silk/ Locust Grove/ Robinson	1	88	c1840	Town	0.7 NW jct US7 on VT67A (Exit 1), then 0.2 left opposite Bennington College campus on Silk Rd.
-05	Sunderland	Roaring Branch, Batten Kill	Chiselville/ High/ Roaring Branch (cement floor)	1+	117	1870	Town	0.2 S jct VT312 (west) on VT7A, then 1.1 left on East Arlington Rd and 1.0 left on Maple St.
Caledonia County								
45-03-01	Danville	Joe's Brook	Greenbank Hollow	1	74	1886	Queen	32.8 W jct VT12B on US2, then 0.8 left (1st turn) and 1.8 right on Joe's Brook Rd. SSE Danville
-03	Lyndon	South Wheelock Branch, Passumpsic River	Schoolhouse/ Chase (closed)	1	42	1879	Queen	0.1 S jct I91 on US5 (Exit 23) (then 0.1 right on bypassed section of South Wheelock Rd.
-04	Lyndon	South Wheelock Branch Passumpsic River	Chamberlin Mill/ Sawmill/ Whjitomb	1	66	1881	Queen	0.2 S jct I91 on US5 (Exit 23) on US5, then 0.3 right and 0.1 left on Chamberlin Bridge Rd. between South Wheelock Rd. and York St.
-05	Lyndon (M1960)	Passumpsic River (closed)	Sanborn/ Centre (private)	1	117	1867	Paddle-ford	0.1 S jct VT114 on W side of US5 adjacent to Lynburke Motel. N edge Lyndonville
-06	Lyndon (RB1995)	Miller's Run	Miller's Run/ Bradley N Lyndon Center	1	56	1878	Queen	1.0 NE jct US5 on VT122. and just left.
-07	Lyndon	E Branch Passumpsic River	Randall/ Old Burrington (closed) (private)	1	68	1865	Queen	1.6 N jct US5 on VT114, then just right on bypassed section of Murray Hill Rd. NE Lyndonville
Chittendon County								
45-04-01	Charlotte	Holmes Creek	Lake Shore/ Holmes	1	41	1870	tied arch	1.3 W jct US7 on VT F-5 through Charlotte, then 1.8 right on Lake Rd.
-02	Charlotte	Lewis Creek Brown's	Upper/ Sequin/	1	71	1850	Burr	2.9 S jct VT2A on VT116, then 1.1 right on Charlotte Rd., 2.4 left on Baldwin Rd., 1.0 right on Drinkwater Rd. and 0.2 left on Roscoe Rd. SW Hinesburg
-03	Charlotte	Lewis Creek	Quinlan/ Lower	1	86	1849	Burr	3.0 E of US7 (opposite SR F-5 on Hinesburg Rd, then 2.1 right on Spear St Extension and just left on Lewis Creek Rd/ S of East Charlotte
-05	Westford (RB 1988)	Brown's River	Westford (closed) (dry land)	1	97	1837	Burr	0.2 E of VT128 on N side of bypassed section of Cambridge Rd.

Number	Township	Stream	Name	Spans	Length	Year	Type	Directions
			(cont'd) Chittendon County					
-06	Shelburne (M1951)	Burr Pond	Cambridge Village/ Museum (admission)	1	168	1845	Burr	5.2 S jct I89 on W side of US7 (Exit 1) on entrance road to Shelburne Museum.
			Essex County - Coos County, NH					
45-05-02 29-04-07	Lemington-Columbia, NH	Connecticut River	Columbia	1	146	1912	Howe	0.3 S of Lemington on US102 and just E.
45-05-03 29-04-08	Lunenburg-Lancaster, NH	Connecticut River	Mount Orne	2	266	1911	Howe	1.5 E of Lunenburg on US2 and 0.3 S on River Rd.
			Franklin County					
45-06-01	Enosburg	Trout River	Hopkins	1	84	1875	Town	2.3 SE jct VT105 on VT118, then just right on Hopkins Rd at Enosburg/Montgomery town line. SE Berkshire
-02	Fairfax	Mill Brook	Village/ Maple Street/ Lower	1	57	1865	Town	0.6 E jct VT128 on VT104, then 0.2 left on Maple St.
-03	Fairfield	Black Creek	East Fairfield (closed)	1	67	1865	Queen	3.2 W jct VT108 on VT36, then 0.1 left on Bridge St. W edge East Fairfield
-04	Montgomery	Trout River	Comstock	1	69	1883	Town	0.4 W of main intersection in Montgomery on VT118, then 0.2 left on Comstock Bridge Rd.
-05	Montgomery RB2001	Black Falls Brook	Fuller/ Black Falls	1	50	1890	Town	0.1 N of VT118 and main intersection in Montgomery on South Richford Rd.
-06	Montgomery	South Branch, Trout River	Hectorville/ Gibou	1	54	1883	Town and King	1.6 S jct VT242 on VT118, then 0.1 right on Gibou Rd.
-07	Montgomery	South Branch, Trout River	Hutchins	1	54	1883	Town	1.2 S jct VT242 on VT118, then 0.3 right on Hutchins Rd.
-08	Montgomery	Trout River Head	Longley/ Harnois/	1	85	1863	Town	1.1 NW of main intersection in Montgomery on VT118, then just left on Longley Bridge Rd.
-09	Montgomery	West Hill Creek	West Hill/ Creamery/ Crystal Springs	1	59	1883	Town	0.5 W of main intersection in Montgomery on VT118, then 2.5 left on West Hill Rd. and 0.2 right on Creamery Bridge Rd.
			Lamoille County					
45-08-01	Cambridge	Brewster River	Scott/ Grist Mill/ Bryant/ Grand Canyon	1	85	1872	Burr	0.5 S jct VT15 on VT108, then 0.1 left on Canyon Rd. S Jeffersonville
-02	Cambridge	Lamoille River	Poland/ Station/ Junction/ Kissing (closed)	1	153	1887	Burr	0.4 N jct VT15 on VT108, then 0.8 right on VT109 and 0.2 right on Poland Bridge R Poland Bridge Rd. At Cambridge Junction
-03	Troy	Missisquoi River	River Road/ School/Upper	1	93	1910	Town	0.1 E jct VT101 on VT100, then 1.1 left on Big Falls Rd.

Number	Township	Stream	Name	Spans	Length	Year	Type	Directions
			(cont'd) Lamoille County					
-04 #2	Cambridge (M1951) (RB 1995)	Seymour River	Little/ Gates Farm (private)	1	60	1897	Burr	0.8 E jct VT104 on VT15, then 0.1 right on farm access road S from VT15.
-06	Belvidere	North Branch, Lamoille River	Lumber Mill	1	71	1895	Queen	6.5 W jct VT118 on VT109, then 0.5 on Black Rd. W Belvidere Center
-07	Belvidere	North Branch Lamoille River	Morgan/ Upper	1	62	1887	Queen	5.6 W jct VT118 on VT109, then just left on Morgan Bridge Rd. W Belvidere Center.
-08	Johnson #2 (RB2002)	Gihon River	Power House/ School Street	1	63	1872	Queen	0.4 E jct VT15 on VT100C, then just left on School St.
-09	Johnson	Gihon River	Scribner DeGoosh	1	48		Queen	1.5 E jct VT15 on VT100C, then 0.3 right and 0.1 right (ahead on Loop Rd. E East Johnson
-11	Morristown	Sterling Brook (cement floor)	Red/ Sterling	1	64	1896	King	1.8 N jct VT108 on VT100, then 0.7 left on Stagecoach Rd, 1.6 left on Sterling Valley Rd. and just right on Cole Rd.
-12	Stowe	Gold Brook	Stowe Hollow/ Gold Brook/ Emily's	1	49	1844	Queen	1.8 S jct VT108 on VT100, then 1.3 left on Gold Brook Rd. and just left on Covered Bridge Rd.
-13	Waterville	North Branch, Lamoille River	Village/ Church Street	1	61	c1877	Queen	4.3 NE jct VT108 on VT109, then 0.1 left on Church St.
-14	Waterville	North Branch, Lamoille River	Montgomery/ Lower/ Potter	1	70	1887	Queen	5.8 NE jct VT108 on VT109, then just right on Montgomery Bridge Rd.
-15	Waterville	North Branch, Lamoille River	Jaynes/ Codding Hollow/ Upper	1	62	c1877	Queen	6.3 NE jct VT108 on VT109, then 0.1 right on Codding Hollow Rd
-16	Wolcott	Lamoille River	Fisher Railroad (steel deck)	1+	98	1908	Town (double)	2.9 W jct VT14 on S side of VT15 in roadside park. W Hardwick
-19	Irasburg	Barton River	Lord's Creek (private)	1	50	1881	Paddle-ford	0.5 E jct VT14 on VT58, then 0.7 left on Covered Bridge Rd.
			Orange County					
45-09-01	Chelsea	1st Branch, White River	Moxley/ Guy	1	56	1883	Queen	2.5 S jct VT13 on VT110, then 0.1 left on Moxley Rd.
-02	Randolph	2nd Branch, White River	Kingsbury/ Hyde	1	46	1904	multiple King	0.4 N of Windsor County line on VT14, then just left on Kingsbury Rd. N East Bethel
-03	Randolph	2nd Branch, White River	Gifford/ C.K. Smith	1	46	1904	multiple King	1.7 S of VT66 on VT14, then 0.1 left on Hyde Rd.

Number	Township	Stream	Name	Spans	Length	Year	Type	Directions
			(cont'd) Orange County					
-04	Randolph	2nd Branch, White River	Johnson/ Braley/ Upper Blaisdell	1	38	1904	multiple King	0.9 S jct US66 on VT14, then 0.1 right on Blaisdell Rd.
-05	Thetford	Ompompa- noosuc River	Union Village	1	111	1867	multiple King variation	2.4 NW jct US5 on VT132, then 0.5 right and just right on Academy Rd. at Union Village
-06	Thetford	Ompompa- noosuc River	Sayres	1+	127		Haupt variation	2.2 NW jct I91 on VT113 (Exit 14), then 0.2 left on Tucker Hill Rd. W edge Thetford Center
-07	Tunbridge	1st Branch, White River	Howe	1	75	1879	multiple King	1.1 N of Windsor County line on VT110, then just right on Belknap Brook (Hill) Rd.
-08	Tunbridge	1st Branch, White River	Cilley/Lower	1	68	1883	multiple King	0.8 SW of Tunbridge village center on VT110, then 0.2 right on Ward Hill Rd.
-09 #2	Tunbridge	1st Branch, White River	Mill/ Hayward	1	76	1883	multiple King	0.1 W VT110 and Tunbridge village center on Howe Ln.
-10	Tunbridge	1st Branch, White River	Larkin	1	68	1902	multiple King	1.0 NE of Tunbridge village center on VT110, then 0.1 right on Larkin Rd.
-11	Tunbridge	1st Branch, White River	Flint	1	87	1845	Queen	3.2 S jct VT113 and Chelsea, then 0.1 left on Bicknell Hill Rd. Just S Chelsea/Tunbridge Town line
			Orleans County					
45-10-01	Irasbug (M1958)	Black River	Orne (private)	1	87	1881	Paddle- ford	0.5 E jct VT14 on VT5, then 0.6 left on W side of Covered Bridge Rd.
			Rutland County					
45-11-02	Brandon	Otter Creek	Sanderson/ Upper	1	132	1840	Town	0.3 SW jct US7/VT73 on Pearl St, then 0.9 right (ahead) on bypassed section of Pearl St. extension.
-03	Clarendon	Mill River	Kingsley/ Mill River	1	121	1870	Town	0.2 E jct VT7B on VT103, then 1.2 right on Airport Rd, 0.2 right on Gorge Rd.
-04	Pittsford- Proctor	Otter Creek	Gorham/ Goodnough	1	115	1842	Town	1.9 S jct US7 on VT3, then 0.5 right on Gorham Bride Rd.
-05	Pittsford	Otter Creek	Hammond	1	145	1843	Town	2.2 NW jct VT3 on US7, then 1.1 left and 0.3 left on bypassed section of Kendall Hill Rd.
-06	Pittsford	Otter Creek	Depot	1	126	1853	Town	1.3 NW jct VT3 on US7, then left and 0.7 left on Depot Rd.
-07	Pittsford	Furnace Brook	Cooley	1	51	1849	Town	1.1 NW jct VT3 on US7 then 1.2 left (2nd turn) on Elm St.
-09	Shrewsbury	Cold River	Brown	1	112	1880	Town	0.4 S jct US4 (west) on US7 and 0.5 right on VT78 to North Clarendon, then 0.7 left to East then 0.7 left to East Rd. intersection, 0.1 ahead to Cold River Rd. 1.6 right and 0.2 left on Upper Cold River Rd (narrow dirt road).

Number	Township	Stream	Name	Spans	Length	Year	Type	Directions
			(cont'd) Rutland County					
-10	Rutland (M1947)	dry land (closed) (private)	Twin	1	60	1850	Town	1.9 N jct US4 (east) on US7, then 0.8 right (ahead) on E side of East Pittsford Rd.
			Washington County					
45-12-02	East Montpelier	Winooski River	Coburn/ Cemetery	1	69	1840s	Queen	2.0 E jct VT14 on US2, then 0.7 left on Coburn Bridge Rd.
-06	Marshfield	Winooski River	Orton Farm/ Martin/Orton (private) (abandoned)	1	45	1890	Queen	1.0 N of main intersection in Plainfield on US2, then just right on farm access road. NE Plainfield
-07	Northfield	Stony Brook	Moseley/ Stony	1	37	1899	King	1.6 SW jct VT12 on VT12A, then 0.2 right and 0.7 left Brook on Stony Brook Rd.
-08	Northfield	Dog River	Station/ Northfield Falls (twin bridge)	1+	137	1872	Town	0.1 W of VT12 and main intersection in Northfield Falls on Cox Brook Rd.
-09	Northfield	Dog River	Slaughter-House	1	60	1872	Queen	0.3 S of main intersection in Northfield Falls on VT12, then 0.1 right on Bailey Rd (St).
-10	Northfield	Cox Brook	Lower/Cox Brook/Newell/ Second (twin bridge)	1	57	1872	Queen	0.2 W of VT12 and main intersection in Northfield Falls on Cox Brook Rd.
-11	Northfield	Cox Brook	Third/ Upper Cox Brook	1	52	c1872	Queen	0.4 W of VT12 and main intersection in Northfield Falls on Cox Brook Rd.
-12	Waitsfield	Pine Brook	Pine Brook/ Wilder	1	48	1872	King	1.2 N of main intersection in Waitsfield on North Rd.
-14	Waitsfield	Mad River	Village/ Big Eddy/ Great Eddy	1	105	1833	Burr	0.1 E of VT100 and main intersection in Waitsfield on Bridge St.
-15	Warren	Mad River	Warren	1	55	1880	Queen	3.4 N of Addison County line on VT100, then 0.4 right and just right on Warren Village Rd.
-18	Barre	Branch of Stevens Brook	Robbins Nest	1	57	1964	Queen	1.7 NW jct VT110 on US302, then just left on private road. NW E Barre
			Windham County					
45-13-01	Brattleboro	Whetstone River	Creamery/ Centerville	1	80	1879	Town	0.3 W jct I91 on VT9 (Exit 2) then just left on Guilford St.
-02	Dummerston	West River	West Dummerston	2	280	1872	Town	7.0 NNW jct US5 on VT30, then just right on East West Rd.
-03	Grafton	South Branch, Saxton's River	Kidder Hill	1	67	1870	King	0.1 E of main intersection in Grafton on VT121, then 0.2 right on Bear Hill Rd. (dead end road).
-04	Guilford	Green River	Green River	1	104	1870	Town	1.4 S jct I91 on US5 (Exit 1), then 4.1 right to Guilford Center, Center, 0.6 ahead, 2.4 right on Jacksonville Stage Rd and 0.1 left, At Green River
-05	Newfane	Rock River	Williamsville	1	118	1870	Town	2.7 W of VT30 and Dummerston-Newfane town line on Dover Road to South Newfane.

Number	Township	Stream	Name	Spans	Length	Year	Type	Directions
			(cont'd) Windham County					
-07 #2	Rockingham	Saxton's River	Hall/ Osgood	1	121	1982	Town	3.2 WNW jct US5 on VT121, then just right on Paradise Hill Rd. E Saxton
-10	Rockingham	William's River	Worrall	1	83	1870	Town	4.5 SE jct VT11 and Chester on VT103, then 0.2 left on Lower Bartonsville Rd. South Bartonsville
-11	Rockingham	William's River	Bartonsville	1	159	1870	Town	4.0 SE jct VT11 and Chester on VT103, then 0.2 left on Pleasant Valley Rd. S edge Bartonsville
-13	Townshend	West River	Scott	3+	276	1870	Town	4.5 SE jct VT100 on VT30, and King then just right on bypassed section of Back Side Rd.
-23	Rockingham (RB1967)	brook	Victorian Village/ Depot (private) (built of materials from -13-12)	1	46	1872	King	2.3 NW jct I91 on VT103, then just left at Vermont Country Store.
			Windsor County					
45-14-01	Hartland	Lull's Brook	Martin's Mill/ Martinsville	1	135	1881	Town	0.4 N jct I91 on US5 (Exit 9), then 0.6 right on Martinsville Rd.
45-14-02	Hartland	Ottauquechee River	Willard/ North Hartland	1	128	1870	Town	0.3 S of Hartland-Quechee Rd. and under I91 on US5, then 0.5 left on Mill Rd. E edge North Hartland
-03	Springfield (M1969)	brook	Baltimore (closed)	1	47	1870	Town	0.9 W jct I91 on US5 (Exit 7), on N side of VT11 in Eureka Schoolhouse Park.
-04	Weathersfield (M1986)	brook	Stoughton/ Titcomb (private)	1	48	1880	multiple King	0.3 S jct VT131 on VT106, then 0.1 left (opposite elementary school) on Andrew Titcomb Farm. S edge Perkinsville
-05	Weathersfield (M1986)	Sherman Brook	Salmond	1	53	c1875	multiple King	2.4 E jct VT106 on VT131, then 0.1 left on old section of Rte 131 (Henry Gould Rd) NE Amsden
-08	Weathersfield	Black River	Upper Falls/ Downer's	1	120	1840	Town	0.3 W jct VT106 on VT44, then 0.1 left on Upper Falls Rd. SW Amsden
-10	West Windsor	Mill Brook	Best/ Swallows	1	37	1889	tied arch	1.3 SE jct VT106 on VT44, then 0.1 right on Churchill Rd. WSW Brownsville
-11	West Windsor	Mill Brook	Bower's/ Brownsville	1	45	c1919	tied arch	1.1 W of main intersection in Brownsville on VT44, then 0.2 right and 0.1 right on Ely Rd. W Brownsville
-12	Woodstock	Ottauquechee River	Taftsville	2	189	1836	multiple King and arch	0.5 W jct VT12 on US4, then 0.1 right on River Rd. Taftsville
-13	Woodstock	Ottauquechee River	Lincoln	1	136	1877	Pratt	3.1 W jct VT106 on US4, just left on Fletcher Hill Rd. SW West Woodstock

Number	Township	Stream	Name	Spans	Length	Year	Type	Directions
	*Windsor County*								
-15	Woodstock	Ottauquechee River	Middle/Union Street	1	139	1969	Town	0.1 W jct VT12 (N) on US4, then just right on Union St.
-17 (1/2 of -08-05)	West Windsor (M1973)	Mill Brook	Twigg-Smith Garfield (private)	1	36	1870	Town	2.4 SE jct VT106 on VT44, then walk 0.1 right on private road. Brownsville
-18 (1/2 of -08-05)	Pomfret (M1973)	Barnard Brook (private)	South Pomfret	1	39	1870	Town	1.1 N jct US4 on VT12, then 1.7 right on South Pomfret-Woodstock Rd. and walk 0.1 left on farm access road. South Pomfret
-116	Woodstock	Gulf Stream	Frank Lewis (private)	1	40	1981	King lattice	3.7 N jct US4 on VT 12. On W side of road.
-117	Hartland	Ottauquechee River						Twin to -14-03
	*Windsor County, VT - Sullivan County, NH*								
45-10-09 29-14-16	Windsor-Cornish, NH	Connecticut River	Windsor-Cornish	2	449	1866	Town	0.3 S jct US44 on US5, then 0.3 W on Bridge St.

VIRGINIA
Alleghany County

Number	Township	Stream	Name	Spans	Length	Year	Type	Directions
46-03-01	Covington	Dunlap Creek	Humpback (closed)	1	100	1857	multiple King	1.2 E jct I64 on US60, then 0.1 right on VT600 in roadside park. W Covington
	*Giles County*								
46-35-01	Newport	Sinking Creek	Sinking Creek	1	70	1916	Queen variation	1.0 ENE jct US460 on VA42, then 0.5 left on W side of bypassed section of VA601.
-02	Newport	Sinking Creek	Link Farm (private)	1	50	1912	Queen variation	1.5 NW jct VA42 (E on US460/VA42), then 0.3 right and 0.1 left on bypassed section of Mountain Lake Rd (VA700).
-03	Newport	Sinking Creek	Red Maple Farm (private) (permission)	1	36	1919	Queen variation	3.5 NW jct US460 on VA42, then walk 0.3 right on private farm road.
	*Patrick County*								
45-68-01	Woolwine	Smith River	Bob White (closed)	2	80	1920	Queen	1.4 S jct VA40 on VA8, then 0.9 left, just right and 0.1 left on bypassed section of VA618
-02	Woolwine	Smith River	Jack's Creek	1	48	1916	Queen	2.3 S jct VA40 on VA8, then 0.2 right on N side of bypassed section of VA615.
	*Rockingham County*								
45-79-01	New Market	Smith Creek	Biedler Farm (private)	1	93	c1800	Burr	0.1 E jct I81 on US211 (Exit 264), then 4.7 right on US11 and 0.6 left on private road opposite VA796 (W).
	*Shenandoah County*								
45-82-01	Mount Jackson	North Fork, Shenandoah (RB1979)	Meem's Bottom River	1+	204	1892	Burr	0.2 E jct I81 on VA730 (Exit 269), then 3.1 right on\ US11 and 0.4 right on VA720.

Number	Township	Stream	Name	Spans	Length	Year	Type	Directions
			WASHINGTON					
			Clark County					
47-06-01	High Valley	Salmon Creek	Milbrandt (private)	1	40	1976	King	E of I5 on 179th St (Exit 9), then 1.0 left on WA502 (NE10th Ave), 11.5 right on 199th St/Risto Rd, 0.2 right on 237th Ave and 0.2 right to end of 206th St at 20806 NE 237th Ave. High Valley
-02	Woodland	Cedar Creek	Lynch/ Grist Mill/ Cedar Creek	1	83	1995	Howe	8 E of Woodland
			Gray's Harbor County					
47-14-01	Montesano	lagoon	Schafer Farm (private)	1	72	1966	Howe	5.0 N of US12/WA8 (State Park exit) through Brady on Middle Satsop Rd to Sharp bend, then left at entrance to Lazy Lama Ranch and right at road fork on road at Carl Schafer Farm Estates.
			King County					
47-17-03	Snoqaulmie	overpass	Salish Lodge (foot)	1	103	1988	Pratt	Between the lodge and the parking lot.
			Lewis County					
47-21-02	Pe Ell	Chehalis River	PeEll (private)	1	65	1934	Howe	2.1 S of WA6 and PeEll on 3rd St/Muller Rd, then just right.
			Wahkiakum County					
47-35-01	Gray's River (RB 1989)	Gray's River	Gray's River	2	158	1905	Howe	2.1 NE jct WA403 on WA4, then 0.2 right on Loop Rd and 0.2 right on Covered Bridge Rd.
			Whitman County					
47-38-01	Colfax	Palouse River	Colfax/Road (private)	1	163	1922	Howe	Just W jct US195 on WA26, then 4.7 right on Green Hollow Rd (CR4370), 0.7 left, on Manning Rd and walk 0.3 left on former railroad right-of-way at Manning Station.
			WEST VIRGINIA					
			Barbour County					
48-01-01	Philippi (RB1989)	Tygart Valley River	Philippi (double) (cement floor)	2+	304	1852	Burr variation	Just E jct US219 on US250.
-02	Carrolton	Buckhannon River	Carrollton (cement floor)	1+	156	1855	Burr	3.4 SSW jct WV57 on US119, then 0.8 left on CR36. E Volga.
			Cabell County					
48-06-01	Milton	Mud River	Milton/ Sink's Mill	1+	148	1876	Howe	0.3 S of I64 on CR13 (Exit 28), then 0.8 right on US60 and 0.3 left on CR25.
			Doddridge County					
48-09-01	Center Point	dry land	Center Point (closed)	1	43	1888	Long variation	On Mud River Rd.

Number	Township	Stream	Name	Spans	Length	Year	Type	Directions
Greenbrier County								
48-13-01	Lewisburg	Milligan Creek	Hern's MIll	1+	54	1884	Queen	3.5 NW jct US219 on US60, then 0.2 left on Bunger's Mill Rd (CR60/11) and 1.1 left on CR40.
-02	Irish Corner	Second Creek	Hoke's Mill (bypassed)	1	82	1899	Long variation	0.4 S jct WV63 (west) on US219, then 3.6 right on CR48 and 1.3 right (ahead) on CR62 (just N of Monroe County line). SW Ronceverte
Harrison County								
48-17-03	Ten Mile	Ten Mile Creek	Fletcher	1	62	1891	multiple King	2.4 W of CR11 (Wolf Summit Exit) on US50, then 1.5 right on CR5 and just left on dead end CR5/29 NNW Wolf Summit
-12	Simpson	Simpson Creek	Simpson Creek/ Hollen Mill	1	79	1881	multiple King	0.2 W of I79 on CR24 (Exit 121) then 0.1 left and just right on bypassed section of CR24/2. NW Bridgeport
Jackson County								
48-18-01	Ravenswood	Left Fork, Sandy Creek	Sarvis Fork	1+	102	1889	Long	3.7 E of I77 (Exit 146), then 3.6 left on CR56, then 2.3 left on CR21 (old US21) and 0.3 right on Sarvis Fork Rd (CR21/15). NE Sandyville
-04	Washington (M1982)	pond	Staat's Mill	1	97	1888	Long	Just N of I77 on CR21 (old US21), then 0.4 right on Cedar Lakes Rd (CR121/26), 2.9 left on CR25 and 0.1 right at entrance to Cedar Lakes FFA/FHA Camp. SE Ripley
Lewis County								
48-21-03	Settlement	Right Fork, West Fork River	Old Red/ Walkersville	1	38	1902	Queen	1.9 N jct WV4 on US19, then just left on road W from US19. S Walkersille
Marion County								
48-25-02	Fairmont	Buffalo Creek	Barrackville (closed)	1	145	1853	Burr	2.0 W jct US19 on US250, then 1.0 right and just ahead on bypassed section of CR250/32.
Monongalia County								
48-31-03	Grant	Dent's Run	Dent's Run/ Laurel Point	1	40	1889	King	5.2 W of WV100 and Westover on US19, then 0.7 right on CR43 and 0.3 left on bypassed section of CR43/6 WNW Laurel Point
Monroe County								
48-32-01	Springfield	Laurel Creek	Laurel Creek/ Lillydale	1	25	1911	Queen	3.3 SW jct WV3 on US219, then 2.9 right on CR219/7 to Lillydale, 1.2 right on CR2193 left on CR219/11 and 0.3 left (ahead) on CR23/4 SW Union

Number	Township	Stream	Name	Spans	Length	Year	Type	Directions
			Monroe County					
-02	Springfield (RB 1965)	Indian Creek	Indian Creek Salt Sulphur Springs (closed)	1	51	1898	Long	4.2 SSW jct WV3 on W side of highway opposite St. John's Church on old Section of US219 in roadside park. SSW Union.
			Pocahontas County					
48-38-01	Little Levels	Locust Creek	Denmar/ Locust Creek	1	116	1870	Warren International double	6.0 SW of US219 and main intersection in Hillsboro, then 0.2 left (ahead) on CR31.
			Wetzel County					
48-52-01	Church	Fish Creek	Hundred/ Fish Creek	1	36	1881	King	0.3 SSE jct WV7 on US250, then 0.1 right on CR13. S edge Hundred

WISCONSIN

Number	Township	Stream	Name	Spans	Length	Year	Type	Directions
			Grant County					
49-22-01	Cassville	Dewey Creek	Stonefield Village (admission)	1	51	1962	Howe	0.4 W jct WI81 and Cassville on WI233, then 1.5 left on CR "VV" to entrance to village on W side of road.
			Ozaukee County					
49-46-01	Cedarburg	Cedar Creek	Cedarburg (closed)	1+	120	1876	Town	1.2 N jct WI60/143 on E side of bypassed section of Covered Bridge Rd.
			Price County					
49-51-01	Chequamegon	South Fork, Flambeau River	Chequamegon/Smith Rapids	1	90	1991	Town	27 W from Minocqua on WI70, then W to Forest Rd 148. Chequamegon National Forest

Index

(The guide starting on page 159 is not included in the following index since it is in alphabetical order by state in its section.)

A

Academia C.B. 119
Ada C.B. 57
Adairs C.B. 124
Al Horton C.B. 14
Al Swann C.B. 14
Amicon C.B. 157

ALABAMA
Blount Co.
  Al Horton C.B. 14
  Al Swann C.B. 14
  Easlel C.B. 15
  Nector C.B. 13
Calhoun Co.
  Coldwater C.B. 15
Cullman Co.
  Clarkson C.B. 15
  Liddy Walker C.B. 15
DeKalb Co.
  Talahatchee/Old Union C.B. 14
  Union/Talahatchee 13
Etowah Co.
  Gilland C.B. 15
Lee Co.
  Salem Shotwell C.B. 15
Talladega Co.
  Waldo/Riddle Mill C.B. 15

Alaman C.B. 23
Albany/Albany C.B. 65
Allegany Park C.B. 70
Americana Village C.B. 70
Amnicon C.B. 157
Anderson Farm C.B. 111
Antelope Creek 89
Aqueduct C.B. 27

B

Baker C.B. 83
Bakers Camp C.B. 36
Banks C.B. 107
Barkhurst C.B. 85
Barlett C.B. 61
Barronvale C.B. 126
Bartonsville C.B. 140
Bath/Bath C.B. 64
Baumgardners C.B. 119
Bay C.B. 87
Bean Blosson C.B. 41
Beaverkill/Conklin C.B. 68
Beech Fork/Mooresville C.B. 50
Beeson C.B. 30
Belknap C.B. 95
Bennett Bean C.B. 52
Bennetts Mill C.B. 51
Bertas Ranch C.B. 17
Bickham C.B. 84
Big Red Oak C.B. 21
Big Rocky Fork C.B. 43
Bigelow C.B. 87
Billie Creek C.B. 30
Bissell C.B. 56
Bistline C.B. 124
Bitzer's Mill C.B. 119
Black Bridge C.B. 55
Black C.B. 82
Blackwood C.B. 72
Blenheim C.B. 68
Bluebird Farm C.B. 82
Bob White C.B. 150
Bogert's C.B. 122
Bollinger Mill C.B. 60
Books C.B. 124
Bowers C.B. 142
Bowmansdale C.B. 117
Bowser/Osterberg C.B. 112
Bowsher C.B. 44
Boy Scout Camp C.B. 75
Bridge at the Green C.B. 143
Bridgeport C.B. 16
Bridgton C.B. 30
Brown C.B. 139
Brownlee C.B. 127
Brubaker C.B. 80
Buchers/Cocalico C.B. 119
Buck Hill C.B. 120
Buckeye Furnace C.B. 84
Bucks/Harrity C.B. 114
Buckskin C.B. 86
Bulls Bridge C.B. 18
Bunker Hill C.B. 130
Burkholder C.B. 126
Busching C.B. 45
Buskirks C.B. 67
Buttonwood C.B. 123
Byer C.B. 83

C

Cabin Run C.B. 100
Cades Mill C.B. 41
Caine Road C.B. 81

CALIFORNIA
Butte Co.
  Castleberry C.B. 16
  Honey Run C.B. 17
Humboldt Co.
  Bertas Ranch C.B. 17
  Brookwood C.B. 3
Mariposa Co.
  Wanowa C.B. 16
Nevada Co.
  Bridgeport C.B. 16
Staneslous Co.
  Knights Ferry C.B. 17
Yuba Co.
  Freemans Crossing C.B. 17

Cambridge Junction C.B. 145
Campbell C.B. 130
Carrollton C.B. 152
Castleberry C.B. 16
Cataract Falls C.B. 29
Catlin C.B. 31
Cavitt C.B. 89
Cedar C.B. 46
Cedar Chapel C.B. 27
Cedar Crossing C.B. 97
Cedarburg C.B. 157
Cemetary C.B. 83
Centennial 96
Centennial C.B. 22
Center Point C.B. 155
Ceylon C.B. 25
Chamberlin C.B. 134
Chambers Road C.B. 82
Charles Harding C.B. 82
Chestnut Creek C.B. 68
Chiselville C.B. 133
Chitwood C.B. 92
Christman C.B. 86
Cilley C.B. 137
Clarkson C.B. 15
Claycomb C.B. 98
Clays Wahneta C.B. 124
Coburn C.B. 147
Cogan House C.B. 123
Coheelee C.B. 21
Coldwater C.B. 15
Colemanville C.B. 105
Colvin C.B. 112
Comstock C.B. 134
Concord C.B. 21
Conleys C.B. 44

CONNECTICUT
Litchfield Co.
  Bulls Bridge C.B. 18
  West Cornwall C.B. 18

Conway Saco River C.B. 61, 62
Cooley C.B. 139
Cornish Windsor C.B. 64
Cornstalk C.B. 36
Cox C.B. 87
Cox Farm C.B. 118
Cox Ford C.B. 31
Coyote Creek C.B. 95
Crawford C.B. 127
Crawfordsville C.B. 97
Creasyville C.B. 115
Creek Road C.B. 81
Cresson/Sawyer C.B. 62
Crooks Bridge C.B. 31
Crystal River C.B. 156
Culbertson C.B. 79
Cumberland C.B. 27
Currin C.B. 90
Cutler Donahoe C.B. 46

D

Dallenburg/Holley C.B. 92
Danley C.B. 110
Darlington C.B. 43
Davis C.B. 115
Davis Farm C.B. 84
Day C.B. 111
Deadwood C.B. 96
Deersmill C.B. 29
Dellville C.B. 124
Delta C.B. 48
Dents Run C.B. 154
Depot C.B. 146
Diehl/Turner C.B. 98
Dixon Branch C.B. 86
Doe Park C.B. 131
Dorena C.B. 90
Dover C.B. 50
Downers/Upper Falls C.B. 142
Downsville C.B. 70
DR Knisley C.B. 112
Dreese/Beavertown C.B. 125
Dreibelbis C.B. 113
Drewsville C.B. 65
Dunbar C.B. 36

E

Eakin Mill C.B. 87
Eames C.B. 23
Earnest Russell C.B. 91
Easlel C.B. 15
Ebenezer C.B. 127
Edna Collins C.B. 45
Eldean C.B. 76
Elders Mill C.B. 21
Enslow C.B. 124
Erbs/Hammer C.B. 120
Erskine C.B. 128
Erwinna C.B. 113
Esther Furnace C.B. 103
Eugene C.B. 45
Euharlee C.B. 20
Everett Road C.B. 87

F

Fairgrounds C.B. 29
Fallsburg C.B. 57
Fish Creek C.B. 155
Fisher RR C.B. 136
Fisher School C.B. 97
Fitches C.B. 67
Fleishers C.B. 124
Fletcher C.B. 76, 154
Flint C.B. 137
Foraker C.B. 77
Forksville C.B. 126
Forry's Mill C.B. 120
Forsythe C.B. 38
Frankenfield C.B. 100
Freemans Crossing C.B. 17

G

Gallon House C.B. 97
Game Reserve C.B. 48
Geeting C.B. 86
Geigers C.B. 122
George Miller C.B. 82

GEORGIA
Banks Co.
  Lula/Blind 13
Bartow Co.
  Euharlee C.B. 20
Cobb Co.
  Concord C.B. 21
DeKalb Co.
  Stone Mountain C.B. 20
Early Co.
  Coheelee C.B. 21
Forsythe Co.
  Pools Mill C.B. 21
Harris Co.
  Wehadkee C.B. 13
Madison/Oglethorpe Co.
  Watson Mill C.B. 21
Meriweather Co.
  Big Red Oak C.B. 21
Oconee Co.
  Elders Mill C.B. 21
Rockdale Co.
  Haralson C.B. 20

Germantown C.B. 84
Giddings Road C.B. 81
Gifford or CK Smith C.B. 138
Gilkey C.B. 97
Gilland C.B. 15
Gilpins C.B. 55
Glenarm C.B. 24
Glessner C.B. 126
Goddard/White C.B. 49
Gold Brook C.B. 145
Goodpasture C.B. 91
Gorham C.B. 146
Grants Mill C.B. 70
Grave Creek C.B. 95
Grays River C.B. 151
Green River C.B. 141
Green Sergeants C.B. 66
Greenbank Hollow C.B. 143
Greenup C.B. 22
Greenway C.B. 75
Greer Mill C.B. 87
Gregg C.B. 76
Greisemer's Mill C.B. 113
Grist Mill/Cedar Creek C.B. 151
Gudgeonville C.B. 117
Guilford C.B. 26
Guy Bard C.B. 120

H

Hall C.B. 141
Halls Mill C.B. 112
Halpin C.B. 143
Hamden C.B. 70
Hammond C.B. 47, 146
Hannah C.B. 93
Haralson C.B. 20
Harmon C.B. 118
Harra C.B. 88
Harry Evan C.B. 44
Harshman C.B. 86
Hartman C.B. 82
Hassenplug C.B. 127
Haverhill C.B. 65
Hayden C.B. 94
Hayes C.B. 127
Hayes Clark C.B. 102
Heikes Farm C.B. 98
Helmick C.B. 73
Helmick Mill C.B. 77
Hemlock C.B. 52
Henry C.B. 128, 133
Herline C.B. 112
Herns Mill C.B. 153
Herrs Mill C.B. 106
Hewitt C.B. 99
Hills C.B. 79
Hillsboro C.B. 51
Hillsdale C.B. 40
Hillsgrove C.B. 127
Hizey C.B. 73
Hoeck C.B. 37
Hoffman C.B. 93
Hokes Mill C.B. 155
Hollingshead C.B. 115
Holliwell C.B. 47
Holton C.B. 38
Hopewell Church C.B. 77
Horse Creek C.B. 94
Horsham C.B. 127
Huffman C.B. 45
Huffman Mill C.B. 39
Huffman Wood C.B. 86
Hughes C.B. 111
Humpback C.B. 149
Hune C.B. 88
Hunseckers Mill C.B. 120
Hunterdon C.B. 66
Hyde South Randolph C.B. 138

I

ILLINOIS
Bureau Co.
  Red C.B. 4
Champaign Co.
  Lake of the Woods C.B. 22
Cumberland Co.
  Greenup C.B. 22
DuPage Co
  Centennial C.B. 22
  Riverwalk Foot C.B. 23

Henderson Co.
  Alaman or Eames CB. 23
Knox Co.
  Wolf C.B. 24
Randolph Co.
  Little Mary's C.B. 24
Sangamon Co.
  Glenarm C.B. 24
Shelby Co.
  Thompson Mill C.B. 24
Imes C.B. 48
Indian Creek C.B. 154

INDIANA
Adams Co.
  Ceylon C.B. 25
Bartholemew Co.
  New Brownsville C.B. 41
Brown Co.
  Bean Blosson C.B. 41
  Ramp Creek C.B. 25
Carroll Co.
  Lancaster C.B. 25
Dearborn Co.
  Guilford C.B. 26
Decatur Co.
  Westport C.B. 26
DeKalb Co.
  Spencerville C.B. 5
Fayette Co.
  Longwood C.B. 26
Fountain Co.
  Cades Mill C.B. 41
  Rob Roy C.B. 42
Franklin Co
  Aqueduct C.B. 27
Franklin Co.
  Snow Hill C.B. 42
Gibson Co.
  Old Red C.B. 42
Grant Co.
  Cumberland C.B. 27
Greene Co.
  Richland Creek C.B. 42
Hamilton Co.
  Cedar Chapel C.B. 27
  Potters C.B. 42
Howard Co.
  Vermont C.B. 42
Jackson Co.
  Medora C.B. 28
  Shieldstown C.B. 42
Jennings Co.
  James C.B. 28
  Sepio C.B. 28
Lake Co.
  Fairgrounds C.B. 29
  Milroy/Crown Point 29
Lawrence Co.
  Williams C.B. 42
Montgomery Co.
  Darlington C.B. 43
  Deersmill C.B. 29
Owen Co.
  Cataract Falls C.B. 29
Parke Co.
  Beeson C.B. 30
  Big Rocky Fork C.B. 43
  Billie Creek C.B. 30
  Bowsher C.B. 44
  Bridgton C.B. 30
  Catlin C.B. 31
  Conleys C.B. 44
  Cox Ford C.B. 31
  Crooks Bridge C.B. 31
  Harry Evan C.B. 44
  Jackson C.B. 44
  Jeffries Ford C.B. 44
  Leatherwood C.B. 32
  Mansfield C.B. 32
  Marshall C.B. 32
  McAllisters Bridge C.B. 44
  Mecca C.B. 33
  Melcher C.B. 33
  Mill Creek C.B. 43
  Narrows Bridge 33
  Neet C.B. 43
  Nevins C.B. 35
  Phillips C.B. 34
  Portland Mills C.B. 34
  Roseville C.B. 43
  Rush Creek C.B. 34
  Sam Smith C.B. 35
  Sanatorium C.B. 43
  Thorpe Ford C.B. 43
  West Union C.B. 45
  Wilkies Mill C.B. 43
  Zacks Cox C.B. 35
Putnam Co.
  Bakers Camp C.B. 36
  Cornstalk C.B. 36
  Dunbar C.B. 36
  Edna Collins C.B. 45
  Hoeck C.B. 37
  Huffman C.B. 45
  Oakkalla C.B. 37
  Pine Bluff C.B. 44
  Rolling Stone C.B. 37
Ripley Co.
  Busching C.B. 45
  Holton C.B. 38
Rush Co.
  Forsythe C.B. 38
  Moscow C.B. 38
  Norris Ford C.B. 39
  Offutt's C.B. 45
  Smith C.B. 39
Scott Co.
  Leota C.B. 45
Spencer Co.
  Huffman Mill C.B. 39
Vermillion Co.
  Eugene C.B. 45
  Hillsdale C.B. 40
  Newport C.B. 40
Vigo Co.
  Irishman C.B. 45
Wabash Co.
  North Manchester C.B. 40
  Roann C.B. 41

IOWA
Cerro Gordo Co.
  Pioneer Park C.B. 48
Keokuk Co.
  Delta C.B. 48
Madison Co.
  Cedar C.B. 46
  Cutler Donahoe C.B. 46
  Hogback C.B. 6
  Holliwell C.B. 47
  Imes C.B. 48
  Roseman C.B. 47
  Roseman covered bridge 3, 11
Marion Co.
  Game Reserve C.B. 48
Muscatine Co.
  Hammond C.B. 47
  Old Marysville C.B. 48
Polk Co.
  Owens C.B. 48
Irishman C.B. 45

J

Jack Mt. C.B. 111
Jacks Creek C.B. 150
Jackson C.B. 44
Jackson Honeymoon C.B. 61
Jackson Mill C.B. 128
Jacksons Mill C.B. 120
Jackson's Mill C.B. 99
James C.B. 28
Jasper C.B. 85
Jaynes "Kissing Bridge" C.B. 136
Jediah C.B. 83
Jeffries Ford C.B. 44
Jerico C.B. 54
Johnson (Braley) C.B. 146
Johnson C.B. 83, 104
Johnson Creek C.B. 51
Johnson Road C.B. 83
Jordan C.B. 94
Josiah Hess C.B. 116
Jud Christian C.B. 116

K

Kaufmans C.B. 120
Keefer Mill C.B. 123
Keefer Station C.B. 123
Kennedy C.B. 114

KENTUCKY
Bourbon Co.
  Colville C.B. 7
Braken Co.
  Walcot/White C.B. 49
Fleming Co.
  Goddard/White C.B. 49
  Hillsboro C.B. 51
  Ringos Mill C.B. 51
Franklin Co.
  Switer C.B. 50
Greenup Co.
  Bennetts Mill C.B. 51
  Oldtown C.B. 51
Mason Co.
  Dover C.B. 50
Robertson Co.
  Johnson Creek C.B. 51
Washington Co.
  Beech Fork/
  Mooresville C.B. 50
Kidder Hill C.B. 148
Kidds Mill C.B. 123
Kidwell C.B. 81
Kings C.B. 126
Kingsley C.B. 146
Kintersberg C.B. 119
Kirker C.B. 80
Klinepeter/Gross C.B. 109
Knechts C.B. 100
Knights Ferry C.B. 17
Knox/Valley Forge C.B. 114
Kochenderfer C.B. 125
Kramer C.B. 104
Krepps C.B. 128
Krickbaum C.B. 123
Kurtz Mill C.B. 106
Kutz C.B. 99

L
Lairdsville C.B. 123
Lake Creek C.B. 96
Lake of the Woods C.B. 22
Lake Shore C.B. 144
Lancaster C.B. 25
Landis Mill C.B. 120
Langley C.B. 59
Larwood C.B. 93
Lawrence Knoebel C.B. 116
Leamans C.B. 121
Leatherman C.B. 128
Leatherwood C.B. 32
Lehmans C.B. 119
Leota C.B. 45
Liddy Walker C.B. 15
Lime Valley C.B. 121
Lincoln C.B. 142
Lincoln Gap C.B. 140
Links Farm C.B. 149
Linton C.B. 114
Little Chucky C.B. 131
Little Gap C.B. 114
Little Mary's C. B. 24
Lockport C.B. 88
Locust Creek C.B. 60, 155
Logan Mill C.B. 115
Long Knowlton C.B. 84
Longley C.B. 135
Longwood C.B. 26
Lost Creek C.B. 95
Loux C.B. 113
Love Joy C.B. 53
Lowell C.B. 96
Lower Humbert C.B. 109
Loys Station C.B. 55
Lyle C.B. 128

M
MAINE
Cumberland Co.
  Bennett Bean C.B. 52
  Hemlock C.B. 52
  Love Joy C.B. 53
  Sunday River C.B. 53
Manassas Guth C.B. 122
Mansfield C.B. 32
Martinsville C.B. 73
Marshall C.B. 32
Martins Mill C.B. 118, 148
Mary Ruffner C.B. 86

MARYLAND
Baltimore/Hackford Co.
  Jerico C.B. 54

Cecil Co.
  Gilpins C.B. 55
Cecil County
  Black Bridge C.B. 55
Frederick Co.
  Loys Station C.B. 55
  Roddy Creek C.B. 54
  Utica C.B. 54

MASSACHUSETTS
Franklin Co.
  Bissell C.B. 56
Worcester Co.
  Service C.B. 56
  Vermont C.B. 56
Mays C.B. 128
McAllisters Bridge C.B. 44
McConnell's Mill C.B. 122
McCracken C.B. 119
McDermott C.B. 65
McGees Mill C.B. 103
McKee C.B. 95
McMillan C.B. 145
Mecca C.B. 33
Medora C.B. 28
Meems C.B. 150
Meiserville C.B. 126
Melcher C.B. 33
Mercers Mill C.B. 115
Mertz C.B. 108

MICHIGAN
Ionia Co.
  Whites C.B. 57
Kent Co.
  Ada C.B. 57
  Fallsburg C.B. 57
Saginaw Co.
  Zehnder C.B. 57
Middle C.B. 143
Middle Road C.B. 80
Mild Academy C.B. 94
Mill Bridge C.B. 136
Mill Creek C.B. 43
Mill Creek/Wendling C.B. 97
Millers Run C.B. 134
Milton Dye C.B. 85
Mink Hollow C.B. 83

MINNESOTA
Goodloe Co.
  Zumbroto C.B. 58

MISSOURI
Cape Girardeau Co.
  Bollinger Mill C.B. 60
Jefferson Co.
  Sandy Creek C.B. 59
Linn Co.
  Locust Creek C.B. 60
Monroe Co.
  Union C.B. 59
St. Joseph Co.
  Langley C.B. 59
Moods C.B. 101
Morgan C.B. 145
Mosby Creek C.B. 96
Moscow C.B. 38
Mount Olive C.B. 87
Moxley C.B. 139
Mt. Pleasant C.B. 125
Museum C.B. 144

N
Narrows Bridge 33
Neddie Woods C.B. 118
Neet C.B. 43
Netcher C.B. 72
Nevins C.B. 35
New Brownsville C.B. 41
New Germantown C.B. 125

NEW HAMPSHIRE
Carroll Co.
  Albany/Albany C.B. 65
  Barlett C.B. 61
  Conway Saco River C.B. 61, 62
  Jackson Honeymoon C.B. 61
Cheshire Co.
  Cresson/Sawyer C.B. 62
  Swanzey/Carleton C.B. 62
  Thompson C.B. 63
  Upper Village C.B. 63

Coos Co.
  Stark/Stark C.B. 63
Grafton Co.
  Bath/Bath C.B. 64
  Haverhill C.B. 65
  Swiftwater C.B. 64
Hillsborough Co.
  Hancock Greenfield C.B. 8
Sullivan Co.
  Cornish Windsor C.B. 64
  Drewsville C.B. 65
  McDermott C.B. 65
  Newport Corbin C.B. 65
New Hope C.B. 72

NEW JERSEY
Hunterdon Co.
  Green Sergeants C. B. 66
  Hunterdon C.B. 66

NEW YORK
Delaware Co.
  Downsville C.B. 70
  Fitches C.B. 67
  Hamden C.B. 70
Herkimer Co.
  Salisbury Ctr. C.B. 67
Madison Co.
  Americana Village C.B. 70
Rensselaer/Washington Co.
  Buskirks C.B. 67
Schoharie
  Blenheim C.B. 68
Stringer Co.
  Allegany Park C.B. 70
Sullivan Co.
  Beaverkill/Conklin C.B. 68
  Chestnut Creek C.B. 68
  Vantran/Livingston C.B. 69
Tompkins Co.
  Newfield C.B. 69
Ulster Co.
  Grants Mill C.B. 70
Washington Co.
  Eaglesville C.B. 9
  Rexleigh C.B. 69
  Shushan C.B. 70
Newell C.B. 147
Newfield C.B. 69
Newport C.B. 40
Newport Corbin C.B. 65
Newton Falls (our old) C.B. 78
Norris Ford C.B. 39

NORTH CAROLINA
Randolph Co.
  Pisgah C.B. 71
North Manchester C.B. 40
North Oriental/Beaver C.B. 126
North Pole C.B. 82

O
Oakkalla C.B. 37
Offutt's C.B. 45

OHIO
Adams Co.
  Kirker C.B. 80
Ashtabula Co.
  Caine Road C.B. 81
  Creek Road C.B. 81
  Doyle Road C.B. 10
  Giddings Road C.B. 81
  Middle Road C.B. 80
  Netcher C.B. 72
  Riverdale C.B. 81
  Root Road C.B. 80
  South Denmark C.B. 81
  State Road C.B. 80
Athens Co.
  Blackwood C.B. 72
  Kidwell C.B. 81
  Palos C.B. 81
Brown Co.
  George Miller C.B. 82
  New Hope C.B. 72
  North Pole C.B. 82

Butler Co.
  Black C.B. 82
Carroll Co.
  Bluebird Farm C.B. 82
Clinton Co.
  Martinsville C.B. 73
Coshocton Co.
  Helmick C.B. 73
Cuyahoga Co.
  Charles Harding C.B. 82
Delaware Co.
  Chambers Road C.B. 82
Fairfield Co.
  Baker C.B. 83
  Hartman C.B. 82
  Hizey C.B. 73
  Johnson C.B. 83
  Mink Hollow C.B. 83
  Rockmill C.B. 74
  Zeller Smith C.B. 74
Greene Co.
  Cemetary C.B. 83
  Stevenson RD C.B. 74
Hamilton Co.
  Jediah C.B. 83
Jackson Co.
  Buckeye Furnace C.B. 84
  Byer C.B. 83
  Johnson Road C.B. 83
Lawrence Co.
  Scott Town C.B. 75
Licking Co.
  Boy Scout Camp C.B. 75
  Davis Farm C.B. 84
  Greenway C.B. 75
  Gregg C.B. 76
  Shoults Girl Scout C.B. 84
Logan Co.
  Bickham C.B. 84
Miami Co.
  Eldean C.B. 76
  Fletcher C.B. 76
Monroe Co.
  Foraker C.B. 77
  Long Knowlton C.B. 84
Montgomery Co
  Germantown C.B. 84
Montgomery Co.
  Jasper C.B. 85
Morgan Co.
  Barkhurst C.B. 85
  Helmick Mill C.B. 77
  Milton Dye C.B. 85
Noble Co.
  Huffman Wood C.B. 86
  Park Hill/Rich Valley C.B. 85
  Parrish C.B. 85
Perry Co.
  Hopewell Church C.B. 77
  Mary Ruffner C.B. 86
  Parks/South C.B. 78
Preble Co.
  Brubaker C.B. 80
  Christman C.B. 86
  Dixon Branch C.B. 86
  Geeting C.B. 86
  Harshman C.B. 86
  Roberts C.B. 78
  Warnke C.B. 86
Ross Co.
  Buckskin C.B. 86
Summitt Co.
  Everett Road C.B. 87
Trumbull Co.
  Newton Falls (our old) C.B. 78
Union Co.
  Bigelow C.B. 87
  Culbertson C.B. 79
  Upper Darby C.B. 87
Vinton Co.
  Bay C.B. 87
  Cox C.B. 87
  Eakin Mill C.B. 87
  Greer Mill C.B. 87
  Mount Olive C.B. 87
Washington Co.
  Harra C.B. 88
  Hills C.B. 79
  Hune C.B. 88
  Rinard C.B. 88
  Root C.B. 88

  Schwenderman C.B. 88
  Shinn C.B. 88
Williams Co.
  Lockport C.B. 88
Wyandot Co.
  Parker C.B. 79
  Swartz C.B. 88
Old Marysville C.B. 48
Old Red C.B. 42
Oldtown C.B. 51

OREGON
Benton Co.
  Hayden C.B. 94
Coos Co.
  Sandy Creek C.B. 89
Deschutes Co.
  Rock O The Range C.B. 94
Douglas Co.
  Cavitt C.B. 89
  Horse Creek C.B. 94
  Mild Academy C.B. 94
  Pass Creek C.B. 95
Jackson Co.
  Antelope Creek 89
  Lost Creek C.B. 95
  McKee C.B. 95
  Wimer C.B. 90
Josephine Co.
  Grave Creek C.B. 95
Lane Co.
  Belknap C.B. 95
  Centennial C.B. 96
  Coyote Creek C.B. 95
  Currin C.B. 90
  Deadwood C.B. 96
  Dorena C.B. 90
  Earnest Russell C.B. 91
  Goodpasture C.B. 91
  Lake Creek C.B. 96
  Lowell C.B. 96
  Mill Creek/Wendling C.B. 97
  Mosby Creek C.B. 96
  Office C.B. 11
  Parvin C.B. 96
  Pengra C.B. 96
  Stewart C.B. 91
  Unity C.B. 96
  Wildcat C.B. 92
Lincoln Co.
  Chitwood C.B. 92
  Fisher School C.B. 97
Linn Co.
  Crawfordsville C.B. 97
  Dallenburg/Holley C.B. 92
  Gilkey C.B. 97
  Hannah C.B. 93
  Hoffman C.B. 93
  Larwood C.B. 93
  Shimanek C.B. 97
  Short C.B. 97
Marion Co.
  Gallon House C.B. 97
  Jordan C.B. 94
Multnoma Co.
  Cedar Crossing C.B. 97
Owens C.B. 48

P
Paar's Mill C.B. 116
Pack Saddle C.B. 110
Palo Alto C.B. 112
Palos C.B. 81
Park Hill/Rich Valley C.B. 85
Parker C.B. 79
Parks/South C.B. 78
Parrish C.B. 85
Parvin C.B. 96
Pass Creek C.B. 95
Patterson C.B. 116
Pengra C.B. 96

PENNSYLVANIA
Adams Co.
  Anderson Farm C.B. 111
  Heikes Farm C.B. 98
  Jack Mt. C.B. 111
  Saucks/Sachs C.B. 112
Beaver Co.
  Woolslayer C.B. 112

Bedford Co,
  Jackson's Mill C.B. 99
Bedford Co.
  Bowser/Osterberg C.B. 112
  Claycomb C.B. 98
  Colvin C.B. 112
  Diehl/Turner C.B. 98
  DR Knisley C.B. 112
  Halls Mill C.B. 112
  Herline C.B. 112
  Hewitt C.B. 99
  Palo Alto C.B. 112
  Raystown/Turner C.B. 113
  Ryot C.B. 113
  Snooks C.B. 113
Berks
  Dreibelbis C.B. 113
Berks Co.
  Greisemer's Mill C.B. 113
  Kutz C.B. 99
  Red/Wertz C.B. 113
Bucks Co.
  Van Sant C.B. 102
Bucks Co,
  Pine Valley C.B. 114
Bucks Co.
  Cabin Run C.B. 100
  Erwinna C.B. 113
  Frankenfield C.B. 100
  Knechts C.B. 100
  Loux C.B. 113
  Moods C.B. 101
  Ralph Stover Park C.B. 101
  Sheards Mill C.B. 114
  Twining Ford C.B. 101
  Uhlerstown C.B. 114
Carbon Co.
  Bucks/Harrity C.B. 114
  Little Gap C.B. 114
Chester Co.
  Hayes Clark C.B. 102
  Kennedy C.B. 114
  Knox/Valley Forge C.B. 114
  Linton C.B. 114
  Rapps Dam C.B. 115
  Sheeder/Hall C.B. 102
  Speakman #1 C.B. 115
  Speakman No. 2 C.B. 103
Chester/Lancaster Co.
  Mercers Mill C.B. 115
  Pine Grove C.B. 115
Clearfield Co.
  McGees Mill C.B. 103
Clinton Co.
  Logan Mill C.B. 115
Columbia & Northumberland Counties
  Richards C.B. 116
Columbia Co.
  Creasyville C.B. 115
  Davis C.B. 115
  Esther Furnace C.B. 103
  Hollingshead C.B. 115
  Johnson C.B. 104
  Josiah Hess C.B. 116
  Jud Christian C.B. 116
  Kramer C.B. 104
  Lawrence Knoebel C.B. 116
  Paar's Mill C.B. 116
  Patterson C.B. 116
  Rupert C.B. 116
  Sam Eckman C.B. 116
  Shoemaker C.B. 117
  Snyder C.B. 117
  Stillwater C.B. 117
  Wanich C.B. 117
  West Paden C.B. 117
Cumberland Co.
  Ramp C.B. 104
Cumberland/York Co.
  Bowmansdale C.B. 117
Erie Co.
  Gudgeonville C.B. 117
  Sherman/Keepville C.B. 117
  Waterford C.B. 118
Franklin Co.
  Martins Mill C.B. 118

229

Witherspoon C.B. 118
Greene Co.
Cox Farm C.B. 118
Neddie Woods C.B. 118
Shriver C.B. 118
White C.B. 118
Huntington Co.
Shade Gap C.B. 105
Indiana Co.
Harmon C.B. 118
Kintersberg C.B. 119
Thomas Ford C.B 105
Trusal C.B. 119
Jefferson Co.
McCracken C.B. 119
Juniata Co.
Academia C.B. 119
Lehmans C.B. 119
Lancaster Co,
Kaufmans C.B. 120
Lancaster Co.
Baumgardners C.B. 119
Bitzer's Mill C.B. 119
Buchers/Cocalico C.B. 119
Buck Hill C.B. 120
Colemanville C.B. 105
Erbs/Hammer C.B. 120
Forry's Mill C.B. 120
Guy Bard C.B. 120
Herrs Mill C.B. 106
Hunseckers Mill C.B. 120
Jacksons Mill C.B. 120
Kurtz C.B. 106
Landis Mill C.B. 120
Leamans C.B. 121
Lime Valley C.B. 121
Pinetown C.B. 121
Pools Forge C.B. 121
Rissers Mill C.B. 121
Schenk's Mill C.B. 121
Shearers Mill C.B. 121
Siegrist Mill C.B. 106
Weavers Mill C.B. 121
White Rock Forge C.B. 122
Willow Hill (Amish) C.B. 122
Zooks Mill C.B. 122
Lawrence Co.
Banks C.B. 107
McConnell's Mill C.B. 122
Lehigh Co.
Bogert's C.B. 122
Geigers C.B. 122
Manassas Guth C.B. 122
Rex C.B. 122
Schlicher C.B. 107
Wehr C.B. 107
Lycoming Co.
Buttonwood C.B. 123
Cogan House C.B. 123
Lairdsville C.B. 123
Mercer Co.
Kidds Mill C.B. 123
Montour Co.
Keefer Mill C.B. 123
Northhampton Co.
Solts/Kriedersville C.B. 109
Northumberland Co.
Keefer Station C.B. 123
Northumberland Co.
Mertz C.B. 108
Rebuck C.B. 123
Rishel C.B. 124
Northumberland/ Columbia Co.
Krickbaum C.B. 123
Northumberland/Montour Co.
Sam Wagner C.B. 108
Perry Co.
Adairs C.B. 124
Bistline C.B. 124
Books C.B. 124
Clays Wahneta C.B. 124
Dellville C.B. 124
Enslow C.B. 124
Fleishers C.B. 124
Kochenderfer C.B. 125

Mt. Pleasant C.B. 125
New Germantown C.B. 125
Rice/Landisburg C.B. 125
Saville C.B. 125
Wagoners C.B. 125
Schuykill Co.
Rock C.B. 108
Shuykill Co.
Zimmermans C.B. 125
Snyder Co.
Klinepeter/Gross C.B. 109
Meiserville C.B. 126
Snyder/Juniata Co.
North Oriental/Beaver C.B. 126
Somerset Co.
Barronvale C.B. 126
Burkholder C.B. 126
Glessner C.B. 126
Kings C.B. 126
Lower Humbert C.B. 109
New Baltimore C.B. 12
Pack Saddle C.B. 110
Shaffer C.B. 110
Trostletown C.B. 126
Sullivan Co.
Forksville C.B. 126
Hillsgrove C.B. 127
Sonestown C.B. 127
Synder Co.
Dreese/Beavertown C.B. 125
Union Co.
Hassenplug C.B. 127
Hayes C.B. 127
Horsham C.B. 127
Washington Co.
Brownlee C.B. 127
Crawford C.B. 127
Danley C.B. 110
Day C.B. 111
Ebenezer C.B. 127
Erskine C.B. 128
Henry C.B. 128
Hughes C.B. 111
Jackson Mill C.B. 128
Krepps C.B. 128
Leatherman C.B. 128
Lyle C.B. 128
Mays C.B. 128
Pine Bank C.B. 129
Plants C.B. 129
Sawhill C.B. 129
Sprowls C.B. 129
Wilson Mill C.B. 129
Wright/Cerl C.B. 129
Phillipi C.B. 152
Phillips C.B. 34
Pigeon C.B. 131
Pine Bank C.B. 129
Pine Bluff C.B. 44
Pine Brook C.B. 147
Pine Grove C.B. 115
Pine Valley C.B. 114
Pinetown C.B. 121
Pioneer Park C.B. 48
Pisgah C.B. 71
Plants C.B. 129
Pools Forge C.B. 121
Pools Mill C.B. 21
Portland Mills C.B. 34
Potters C.B. 42
Power House C.B. 145
Pulp Mill C.B. 132

Q
Quechee C.B. 148
Quinlan C.B. 144

R
Ralph Stover Park C.B. 101
Ramp C.B. 104
Ramp Creek C.B. 25
Randall C.B. 144
Rapps Dam C.B. 115
Raystown/Turner C.B. 113
Rebuck C.B. 123
Red Bridge C.B. 137
Red/Wertz C.B. 113
Rex C.B. 122
Rexleigh C.B. 69
Rice/Landisburg C.B. 125
Richards C.B. 116
Richland Creek C.B. 42

Rinard C.B. 88
Ringos Mill C.B. 51
Rishel C.B. 124
Rissers Mill C.B. 121
River Road School House C.B. 138
Riverdale C.B. 81
Riverwalk Foot C.B. 23
Roann C.B. 41
Rob Roy C.B. 42
Roberts C.B. 78
Rock C.B. 108
Rock O The Range C.B. 94
Rockmill C.B. 74
Roddy Creek C.B. 54
Rolling Stone C.B. 37
Root C.B. 88
Root Road C.B. 80
Roseman C.B. 47
Roseville C.B. 43
Rupert C.B. 116
Rush Creek C.B. 34
Ryot C.B. 113

S
Salem Shotwell C.B. 15
Salisbury Ctr. C.B. 67
Salisbury Station C.B. 132
Salmond C.B. 148
Sam Eckman C.B. 116
Sam Smith C.B. 35
Sam Wagner C.B. 108
Sanatorium C.B. 43
Sanborn C.B. 144
Sandy Creek C.B. 59, 89
Sarvis Fork C.B. 155
Saucks/Sachs C.B. 112
Saville C.B. 125
Sawhill C.B. 129
Sayers/Haupt C.B. 146
SCHAFERS C.B. 151
Schenk's Mill C.B. 121
Schlicher C.B. 107
School House C.B. 144
Schwenderman C.B. 88
Scott Grist Mill C.B. 145
Scott Town C.B. 75
Sepio C.B. 28
Service C.B. 56
Shade Gap C.B. 105
Shaffer C.B. 110
Sheards Mill C.B. 114
Shearers Mill C.B. 121
Sheeder/Hall C.B. 102
Sherman/Keepville C.B. 117
Shieldstown C.B. 42
Shimanek C.B. 97
Shinn C.B. 88
Shoemaker C.B. 117
Shoreham/Rutland RR C.B. 132
Short C.B. 97
Shoults Girl Scout C.B. 84
Shriver C.B. 118
Shushan C.B. 70
Siegrist Mill C.B. 106
Silk Road C.B. 133
Simpson Creek C.B. 152
Sinking Creek C.B. 149
Smith C.B. 39
Smith Rapids C.B. 156
Snooks C.B. 113
Snow Hill C.B. 42
Snyder C.B. 117
Solts/Kriedersville C.B. 109
Sonestown C.B. 127
South Carolina
Catawba Co.
Bunker Hill C.B. 130
Greenville Co.
Campbell C.B. 130
South Denmark C.B. 81
Spade Farm C.B. 143
Speakman #1 C.B. 115
Speakman No. 2 C.B. 103
Springwater C.B. 156
Sprowls C.B. 129
Staats Mill C.B. 153
Stark/Stark C.B. 63
State Road C.B. 80
Station C.B. 140
Stevenson RD C.B. 74
Stewart C.B. 91
Stillwater C.B. 117
Stone Mountain C.B. 20

Sunday River C.B. 53
Swanzey/Carleton C.B. 62
Swartz C.B. 88
Swiftwater C.B. 64
Switer C.B. 50

T
Taftsville C.B. 148
Talahatchee/Old Union C.B. 14

TENNESSEE
Carter Co.
Doe Park C.B. 131
Greene Co.
Little Chucky C.B. 131
Sevier Co.
Pigeon C.B. 131
Thomas Ford C.B. 105
Thompson C.B. 63
Thompson Mill C.B. 24
Thorpe Ford C.B. 43
Trostletown C.B. 126
Trusal C.B. 119
Twining Ford C.B. 101

U
Uhlerstown C.B. 114
Union C.B. 59
Union Village C.B. 147
Unity C.B. 96
Upper Cox C.B. 147
Upper Darby C.B. 87
Upper Seguin C.B. 144
Upper Village C.B. 63
Utica C.B. 54

V
Van Sant C.B. 102
Vantran/Livingston C.B. 69

VERMONT
Willard C.B. 147
Addison Co.
Halpin C.B. 143
Pulp Mill C.B. 132
Salisbury Station C.B. 132
Shoreham/Rutland RR C.B. 132
Spade Farm C.B. 143
Bennington Co.
Bridge at the Green C.B. 143
Chiselville C.B. 133
Henry C.B. 133
Silk Road C.B. 133
Caledonia Co.
Chamberlin C.B. 134
Greenbank Hollow C.B. 143
Millers Run C.B. 134
Randall C.B. 144
Sanborn C.B. 144
School House C.B. 144
Chittendon Co.
Lake Shore C.B. 144
Museum C.B. 144
Quinlan C.B. 144
Upper Seguin C.B. 144
Franklin Co.
Cambridge Junction C.B. 145
Comstock C.B. 134
Longley C.B. 135
Village C.B. 135
Village/Maple St. C.B. 145
Lamoille Co.
Fisher RR C.B. 136
Gold Brook C.B. 145
Jaynes "Kissing Bridge" C.B. 136
Mill Bridge C.B. 136
Morgan C.B. 145
Power House C.B. 145
Red Bridge C.B. 137
Scott Grist Mill C.B. 145
Waterville C.B. 135
Orange Co.
Cilley C.B. 137
Flint C.B. 137
Gifford or CK Smith C.B. 138

Hyde South Randolph C.B. 138
Johnson (Braley) C.B. 146
Moxley C.B. 139
Sayers/Haupt C.B. 146
Union Village C.B. 147
Orleans Co.
River Road School House C.B. 138
Rutland Co.
Brown C.B. 139
Cooley C.B. 139
Depot C.B. 146
Gorham C.B. 146
Hammond C.B. 146
Kingsley C.B. 146
Washington Co.
Coburn C.B. 147
Lincoln Gap C.B. 140
Newell C.B. 147
Pine Brook C.B. 147
Station C.B. 140
Upper Cox C.B. 147
Windham Co.
Bartonsville C.B. 140
Creamery C.B. 13
Green River C.B. 141
Hall C.B. 141
Kidder Hill C.B. 148
McMillan C.B. 145
West Dummerston C.B. 141
Williamsville C.B. 148
Worrall C.B. 148
Windsor Co
Downers/Upper Falls C.B. 142
Windsor Co.
Bowers C.B. 142
Lincoln C.B. 142
Martins Mill C.B. 148
Middle C.B. 143
Quechee C.B. 148
Salmond C.B. 148
Taftsville C.B. 148
Vermont C.B. 42, 56
Village C.B. 135
Village/Maple St. C.B. 145

VIRGINIA
Alleghany Co.
Humpback C.B. 149
Giles Co.
Links Farm C.B. 149
Sinking Creek C.B. 149
Patrick Co.
Bob White C.B. 150
Jacks Creek C.B. 150
Shenandoah Co.
Meems C.B. 150

W
Wagoners C.B. 125
Walcot/White C.B. 49
Waldo/Riddle Mill C.B. 15
Walkersville C.B. 153
Wanich C.B. 117
Wanowa C.B. 16
Warnke C.B. 86

WASHINGTON
Clarke Co.
Grist Mill/Cedar Creek C.B. 151
Grays Harbor Co.
Schafers C.B. 151
Wahkiakum Co.
Grays River C.B. 151
Waterford C.B. 118
Waterville C.B. 135
Watson Mill C.B. 21
Weavers Mill C.B. 121
Wehr C.B. 107
West Cornwall C.B. 18
West Dummerston C.B. 141
West Paden C.B. 117
West Union C.B. 45

WEST VIRGINIA
Barbour Co.
Carrollton C.B. 152
Phillipi C.B. 152
Doddridge Co.
Center Point C.B. 155

Greenbriar Co.
Hokes Mill C.B. 155
Greenbrier Co.
Herns Mill C.B. 153
Harrison Co.
Fletcher C.B. 154
Simpson Creek C.B. 152
Jackson Co.
Sarvis Fork C.B. 155
Staats Mill C.B. 153
Lewis Co.
Walkersville C.B. 153
Long Monroe Co.
Indian Creek C.B. 154
Monogalia Co.
Dents Run C.B. 154
Pocahontas Co.
Locust Creek C.B. 155
Wetzel Co.
Fish Creek C.B. 155
Westport C.B. 26
White C.B. 118
White Rock Forge C.B. 122
Whites C.B. 57
Wildcat C.B. 92
Wilkies Mill C.B. 43
Willard C.B. 147
Williams C.B. 42
Williamsville C.B. 148
Willow Hill (Amish) C.B. 122
Wilson Mill C.B. 129
Wimer C.B. 90

WISCONSIN
Amnicon C.B. 157
Price Co.
Smith Rapids C.B. 156
Washington Co.
Cedarburg C.B. 157
Waushara Co.
Crystal River C.B. 156
Winnebao Co.
Springwater C.B. 156
Witherspoon C.B. 118
Wolf C.B. 24
Woolslayer C.B. 112
Worrall C.B. 148
Wright/Cerl C.B. 129

Z
Zacks Cox C.B. 35
Zehnder C.B. 57
Zeller Smith C.B. 74
Zimmermans C.B. 125
Zooks Mill C.B. 122
Zumbroto C.B. 58

230